# Down Memory Line

## The Sligo Leitrim & Northern Counties Railway

Michael Hamilton

# Dedication

*I would like to dedicate this book to my wife Florence, for her help and encouragement; also to the Railway men and women, who gave long working years to the SL & NCR*

Michael Hamilton

# Down Memory Line

## The Sligo Leitrim & Northern Counties Railway

First published in Ireland in 1997 by
Drumlin Publications, Manorhamilton, Co. Leitrim

© Michael Hamilton 1997

ISBN 1 873437 18 8

**Published by Drumlin Publications, Nure,
Manorhamilton, Co. Leitrim, Ireland (072) 55237**
Front cover Photo: N.Sprinks
Layout & Design by Daragh Stewart
Printed by Colour Books, Dublin

# Acknowledgements

Grateful thanks is extended to Michael Davies, Dave Murray, Jack McGoldrick, Mrs Kathleen Hosie, Harold Johnston, Michael Kennedy, Dave Parkes, Maureen Keaney and R.K.Walton for sharing with me some photos and memorabilia.

Also to Michael Kearins, Mrs Margaret Carty, Mairéad O Dolan, Pauric McKeon, Harold Thompson, for their helpful railway information, which I am most grateful for and to Prin and Betty Duignan for their support.

# Contents

SL&NCR Railway Map

# Preface

I invite you to come with me on a train journey into the west. At Enniskillen station stands the SL&NCR 7.20pm Sligo steam train, at departure platform No. 1. So on this summer's evening, come on board and travel with me, the guard, through the beautiful country-side to Sligo. All aboard!

Immediately we cross over the Tempo Road bridge and are heading into the enchanting Castlecoole wood with its lovely overhanging trees which shelter us for a moment from the hot summer's sun. We are now approaching the magnificent Weirs bridge (often called the Killyhevlin bridge) which spans the River Erne. We are moving slow-ly for the speed limit for crossing is just 5m.p.h. We get an opportuni-ty from our carriage windows to enjoy a breath taking view of this peaceful river which joins Upper and Lower Lough Erne. Two wild duck, frightened by the approach of our train, hurriedly take off into the air, leaving a narrow   ripple on the calm waters. Fishermen lazily cast their fishing lines from their boats while many people sit leisure-ly on the banks. On our left we can see the Killyhevlin hotel tucked into its surrounding woods. On the the bank, cattle rest and chew their cud. As I stand beneath the veranda of my guard's van I can see Coles' Monument back in the distance. Passing No. I level crossing we can see on our left part of Lisgoole Abbey.

As we roll into Florencecourt with its beautiful cut stone single storey building we are greeted by Archie Burns the station master, dressed in full uniform. On leaving here we travel through flat country with fine tilled fields. On our left as we approach Belcoo, our train runs along the shores of Lower Lough Macnean and across its waters we can see the 'hanging rock' and the Marble Arch where the world renowned underground caves can be explored. It is 7.55pm as we enter Belcoo station where H.M. customs conduct an examination of all passengers' luggage.

Heading for Glenfarne we cross the 'border' river which connects Upper and Lower Macnean. Travelling along the shore of the upper lake we can see Holywell church nestling into the hillside. A short distance on, Killinagh old church and graveyard come into view while on our left stand the Methodist church and the Church of Ireland. As we pass the White Fathers College (now Loughan House prison) we see to our left Killinagh Catholic church. Rugged country lies ahead of us before we enter Glenfarne station where there is another customs check, this time by Irish officers. We leave Glenfarne at 8.10pm and make our way by hill and valley to the area known as the 'Big Bog'.

Past Killmackerrill halt, the train speeds on through Lisnagroagh and Cherrybrook from where there is a clear fall all the way into Manorhamilton. The driver fills the engine water tank here and as the clock shows 8.30pm we pull out of the station heading for Dromahaire. We journey between two mountains, Benbo on our right and Raymore on our left. In the distant meadow fields the farmers are saving the hay. They wave their hats to us as we pass by. Further on, the meadows are closer and we can sense the urgency of the workers as the dew begins to fall. The women wearing headscarves and floral cross-over aprons are raking in the hay. They smile at us and raise their rakes in salute. The men do likewise with their hayforks. A horse harnessed to a hay raker shuffles nervously as we pass. In a corner of the meadow hay rope making is in progress. A man down on one knee, his straw hat set at a funny angle, is feeding out the coarse hay as a young boy does the twisting. Now we are running along with the river Bonet to our right. On our left is the Manorhamilton-Drumkeerin road. We leave behind Soxline and ease into Dromahaire. This is the only two-storey station building on the line.

Departing at 8.50pm we immediately move through a beautiful avenue of beech-trees for almost three quarters of a mile and then into the townlands of Edergole, Derrybrisk (on our left is the famous Spa well), Tobernania and Ailveiled. We don't stop today in Ballintogher for we have received no request to do so. Having surmounted the hill in the townland of Woodfield we descend all the way into Collooney. On our right are the ruins of Drumcondra Castle. Before we pass Ballygawley halt in the townland of Castledargan, we can see the spire of Collooney church.

A five minute shunt has to be made in order to detach some empty cattle wagons from our train. At 9.15pm we leave the station and cross the Owenmore river. On our left is the spur line which connects the SL&NCR with the Collooney/Claremorris/Limerick line. We pass in sight of Teeling's monument and head through flat country running parallel with the C.I.E. main line from Carrignagat to Ballisodare station, where our train crosses over onto the main C.I.E. down line.

It is 9.25pm as we pull out of Ballisodare; we pass over Ballidreid bridge and take in the lovely view of Ballisodare bay with its rising tidal waters. Far out, the late evening sun casts an orange glow on the waters. Straight ahead is Knocknarea where the legendary Queen Maeve is buried. As we near Sligo, the driver reduces speed for the gradual fall into the station. Our train comes to a halt at 9.35pm. We alight on the glass roofed platform and the setting sun throws long shadows onto the biscuit-coloured walls. But this was a journey of yesteryear – only a memory to lock away and treasure.

Myself and my brother Tommy,
at Derry-Brisk, Dromahaire in 1937.

My father James on the tracks,
at Derry-Brisk, Dromahaire.

The Sir Henry hauling goods wagons. Photo: N.Sprinks

# CHAPTER ONE

# A Railway Family

Growing up as a boy on the railway was a fascinating experience for me. My parents lived in a level crossing gatehouse, in the townland of Derrybrisk, which was built on my paternal grandfather's land, some of which had been acquired and purchased in 1880 by the Sligo, Leitrim and Northern Counties Railway [S.L. & N.C.R.] for the laying of the new track. My grandfather joined the railway in 1888 and worked as a milesman until his death in 1927. A milesman's duties entailed maintaining the track and securing the railway fences against 'thieving' cattle. My other grandfather, Charlie Carty and his son (named Charlie as well) worked as milesmen as did my own father, James, who was still with the railway when it closed in 1957. My Uncle Thomas was employed as an engine fireman. So it was no surprise that my boyhood ambition was to work on the railway, hoping eventually to become a fireman or engine-driver.

The speed and power of the heavy cattle and goods trains as they thundered past our door will always live in my memory. My favourite engine was the *Sir Henry*, because of its great size, and I often watched it climb the steep hill beyond our house, steam shivering from its sides as it pulled the goods train onwards to Sligo. Sometimes, when we as children heard a goods train in the distance we would dash beneath the nearby river bridge to hear the rattle of the carriages above our heads.

Apart from watching the trains, my favourite pastime was fishing. It was my father who taught me the art. He used to make up his own fishing equipment. First he selected and cut a straight, long, hazel rod, then attached a brown line and an eye-hook. A small piece of lead did the work of a 'sinker' while a bottle-cork acted as a 'marker'. Whenever a big flood came down the river we would set off. The river ran parallel with the railway line and so I could enjoy the fishing and watch the trains go by at the same time. Before we left the bank, my father would get a forked stick and run it through the gills of the brown trout – this was a handy way to carry them home.

Many people going to Dromahaire to do their shopping passed through the level crossing gates at our house. On their way back home, they often called in to my mother to 'céilí' for a while. My mother always made tea for them. In our kitchen there was a big crane built into the open fireplace and on it a black kettle was always on the boil – tea making was instant in our house. The visitors, before leaving, always produced the 'bag of sweets' which my mother shared out among us and because we were always looking for more, she would say, "Ye won't have tooth left in your heads before ye grow up". Friday, the ten-shilling pension day was a great day for sweets. Our favourites were 'pink smokers' – round and small with a sweet smell.

Sometimes people would say to my mother "How can you rear your children so close to the railway tracks?". Indeed our parents continually warned us not to go onto the line but to play in the nearby fields. My brother Tommy came close to being killed when he was aged about three. He wandered out onto the tracks and was sitting there as a train approached. Luckily he was wearing a red jersey which attracted the notice of a gang of milesmen who were working further up the line. One of them, Francie Leahy, who was a very athletic man, raced towards him and snatched him to safety out of the path of the oncoming train.

My mother managed with a fair degree of success to rear a large number (approximately ninety) of hens, something which amazed the Permanent Way Inspector, William McBride from Lurganboy.

"How on earth, Mrs Hamilton, can you mind such a big flock of hens, which I see spend most of their time on the tracks," he once asked her.

"It's a bit of a problem alright, some of them do get killed, as many as two or three at a time," mother replied.

Very few hens were killed by the steam trains, as the noise of their approach could be heard a distance away thus giving time to clear the birds off the tracks. However, when the quieter rail cars were introduced in 1935, the casualty rate was much higher.

There was no shortage of food for the hens. They were fed on potatoes and oats grown by my father. The oats was brought down to the local Breffni Creamery for crushing. The crushed oats, mixed with boiled potatoes, ensured that the hens would lay 'out of face'. My mother reared four breeds – *Rhode Island Reds, Anchoras, White Wyandots* and *White Leghorns*. She bought most of the hatching eggs from Mrs Winifred Kelly, who had an egg hatchery in Dromahaire. Another supplier was Mrs 'Bob Harry' Hamilton, a dear old lady who always put in fourteen eggs instead of a dozen in case there were any 'blanks'.

Some of the chickens, when around five weeks old, were liable to pick up a disease we called the 'pip', for which there was a very effective local cure. A small handful of lime was put into an empty shoe box and a hole big enough to hold the connection of a bicycle pump was made in the side. Then, after the sick chicken was placed in the box the lid was tightly sealed. Air was pumped into the box with a bicycle pump to ensure that the chicken inhaled lime-mixed air. Usually the bird was back to full health in a couple of days.

The old hens were bought by John Moran, a dealer from Sligo. My mother sold him five or six each time he called – four shillings for a good hen and two and six for an inferior specimen. John carried the hens in two crates which were affixed to the front carrier of his messengerboy type bicycle. Then it was back to Sligo with him, cycling on roads which were untarred. John's brother, Eddie was engaged in the same trade in the Templeboy/Skreen area of Co. Sligo.

On one occasion my mother had gone to Dromahaire to do the shopping when John called. My sister Kathleen and I were left in charge of the house. John called out as he neared the house.

"Any old hens for sale?"

Kathleen and I decided to sell him one hen and keep the money. We grabbed a hen out in the street and John handed over two and six. The following day my mother counted her hens, as she did occasionally.

She was shocked to find that one of her best laying hens was missing. Guilt was written all over our faces and the truth, and nothing but the truth, was demanded. The real pain was that all the money was taken back by my mother. John, I'm sure, was delighted with the bargain.

John Byrne from Tully was the egg buyer in our area. He used to call every Friday with his travelling shop, drawn by a lazy white horse. At peak laying time my mother would have twenty five dozen eggs for sale which she carried out to him in two baskets after he halted at the railway gates. John counted and examined the eggs before he put them into sections of a big wooden box. Then he scribbled on a piece of brown paper as he worked out the price of the eggs. My mother then bought items from the shop after the sale was completed. These included tea, sugar, currants, bread, *Breffni Blossom* jam, two ounces of *Murray's Twist* tobacco for my father and paraffin oil, which John stored in a big barrel tied beneath the floor of the vehicle. Mrs Torsney, who lived nearby, also came to the railway gates to sell her eggs and purchase groceries. She and my mother and John would chat for awhile and exchange the local gossip. If a train approached John would climb down from his shop to hold the horse's head until the train sped past.

Saturday morning was butter making time in our house and my sister Kathleen, Tommy my brother and I were expected to take a hand at the churning – a task we dared not avoid. When the churning was over my mother took off all the butter which was floating on the buttermilk and with her butter spades she made it into beautiful prints. If the butter looked pale she added some carrot juice to give it a nice golden colour. The carrot was from our vegetable garden at the back of the house. After cleaning and grating the carrots she extracted the juice. The buttermilk was beautiful and we loved to drink it when taking our dinner. It was also used for baking soda bread and any surplus was fed to the young calves on the farm. Coming towards the end of the autumn, the churning would slow down as the cows would not be producing the same volume of milk as in the summer months. When milk was scarce in the winter, my mother would often send me up for some buttermilk to my god-mother, Mary Fowley, who lived about a mile from our house, in the townland of Drumrane. I used to set off with my 'sweetcan' as it was known. On arrival at the house I would be welcomed by Mary, who filled the can with buttermilk from a big urn she kept in the 'parlour' room. After making tea for me she would follow me out to the cobbled street and press a shilling into my fist. Later, mother would take the lid off the can to discover a beautiful print of butter floating on top of the buttermilk, which Mary had generously given for the use of our family.

Also on Saturday, Josie Baker, the Riverstown butcher delivered fresh meat to our house. He came aboard his springcart, drawn by a black pony. A bell was attached to the pony's collar and it could be heard a mile away as he trotted along. We, as children, would be on the look-out for Josie and as soon as we heard the bell we would rush into the kitchen shouting: "Josie Baker is on his way". Then running along the tracks to the Black railway gate we would climb over the accommodation style onto a narrow boreen, join Josie at Dan Rourke's crossroads and escort him to our house where my mother would purchase fresh meat for Sunday's dinner. Another butcher, who sold meat in our district, was Martin Lane from Ballintogher. He was a big man who specialised in mutton, which he transported by bicycle.

SL&NCR Workmen and staff at Manorhamilton, 1925.

Those identified: 1.'Toastie' Keaney, 2.Jimmy Dunbar, 3.Jack McGoey, 4.Johnny Thompson(sign-writer), 5.Pat Dolan, 6.Harry Gray, 7.Pat Darcy, 8.Dominic Connolly(clerk), 9.Gerry Lamb, 10.Ernie Monaghan, 11.Willie Gray, 12.Tommy Rutherford, 13. Jimmy Renwick, 14.Mr.R.W.Sparks, 15.Pat Keaney, 16.Bob Belford.

# CHAPTER TWO

# Entertainment in the Country

During the winter months card playing was the commonest pastime in our house. About eight players would take part a couple of times a week. The first to arrive, usually, was Charlie Loughlin, a distant relation of ours. At approximately half four in the evening he used to lift the door-latch, walk in and say, "God bless all who dwell in this house." He then would head for the fireplace and sit on a cosy stool before a bright, open fire. He stayed in that position until about six o'clock, when on the invitation of my mother, he moved to the table to have tea and baked soda bread, smothered in country butter.

"You're a great hand at the baking. Wasn't James Hamilton the lucky man to get you," he'd say.

By this time my father would be home from work and he would join Charlie at the table. After the tea, Charlie resumed his seat at the fireside and usually had a wee snooze until the arrival of the card players at around eight o'clock. The kitchen table was then pulled out to facilitate the players. Sometimes arguments would arise and our local schoolteacher Eugene Mullhooley would intervene with, "Cool it down lads". This usually had a calming effect on the others. One of the players, Tom Gallagher, had a reputation of being mean. If he dropped a halfpenny on the floor he would go on all fours searching for it until one of the lads would advise him,

"Will you get up off your knees. You have enough praying done-leave it to the house sweeper."

My father took part in a few games only, because he had to attend to the level crossing gates at five to nine, shortly before the last train was due to pass. As it sped past the whole house shook. My father stood in the doorway for the notices, which the guard threw to him from the moving train. These notices contained information on special trains etc. After passing our house the train had to ascend a steep incline and, as it struggled to the top, showers of sparks from its chimney would shoot into the night sky and drop again like falling stars. When my father had opened the gates again to road traffic, he quenched the gate lamp and the signal lamps and secured them for the following day.

"It's time now lads for the last game," he used to tell the card players at ten o'clock.

"Double your stakes for this one and call it a day. I have to be up early in the morning to open the gates for the twenty past six rail car from Sligo."

They would then leave, Charlie being the last with his pocket flashlamp showing the way home.

If a storm arose during the night the railway would have to be 'walked' or inspected for fallen trees or branches before the Sligo railcar was due to pass. This was very necessary, on our section of the line, because the trains passed through a beech plantation, which extended for about a mile down to Dromahaire station. My uncle, Charlie Carty, had the responsibility of going out in the dark morning hours to clear the tracks. It sometimes happened that a tree had fallen and he would then get my father to assist him in sawing and removing the tree before the approach of the railcar. Saws and cross-cuts were kept in the black wooden tool box near our house.

I always associate the dark winter nights with the fairy fort *Moneen Rua* and I remember well when I first saw its fairy lights. One evening in late November after my father arrived home from work my mother told him that there weren't many potatoes left in the sack out in the shed. This meant that he would have to go up to the potato pit which was three quarters of a mile away on a lonely bleak hill.

"I'll go up and fetch some," my father said. I'll take Michael with me to hold the sack while I fill it. On second thoughts I'd best wait until the Enniskillen goods train has passed and I'll take the railway lamp with me."

When the train passed, in all its fury and won its battle over the steep incline, we set off for the potato pit, first by a narrow boreen and then onto the hillside. My father opened the face of the pit while I held open the mouth of the sack as the oil lamp gave us the necessary light. To our left in the dim moonlight we could see in the distance *Moneen Rua*, the fairy fort, with its weaving lights moving in rings all around. As we moved down the hill out of sight of the lights of the dancing fairies I was still bewildered by the experience. As my father carried the sack of potatoes on his shoulders, he told me that many a time he heard beautiful music coming out of the fort. *Moneen Rua* is still the same today with its two storm battered whitethorn bushes.

"Thank God the fair in Dromahaire is over for another month," was a favourite saying of my mother, who dreaded the problems presented by the cattle and their owners at the level crossing gates. From early morning the farmers were on the move – from Greaghnafarna, Clerhan and Drumrane. When a train was due to pass the gates were closed to road traffic and the cattle, crowded on the road, often grew restless. Sometimes they broke into the plantation and onto side roads. My mother was always afraid that they might burst onto the tracks and cause a major accident. Sometimes the owners would be shouting and roaring in anger and frustration. Occasionally my mother took a chance and opened the gates to let the cattle through, having first set the warning signals for trains at 'Danger'. The signal for trains coming from Enniskillen was positioned only a quarter of a mile from the gates, while the Sligo signal was three-quarters of a mile distant. As a child I was always fascinated by the huge number of cattle passing through. They were mostly black in colour but now and again you would spot a *'Kerry Cow'* among them. Some farmers, in order to iden-tify their own cattle, often tied different coloured ribbons to their tails.

If cattle were not sold at the fair, there would be a reoccurrence of the trouble at the gates in the the evening. This was especially true in the winter months as darkness set in early. The farmers would be bring-ing their animals home from about four o'clock onwards. When my father came home from work, my mother was relieved to hand over to him the responsibility of getting the cattle safely through the gates.

The radio and gramophone played important roles in my childhood as far as entertainment was concerned. The Torsneys, who lived close to us, had the only radio in the locality and for programmes such as *'Question Time'*, their house would be full, with some people even sitting on the stairway. On *All-Ireland Final Day* the street outside the house was packed. The radio, which was operated by wet and dry batteries, had the name *'Cossar'* written on it. After a match, some people would go to our house for a céilí and always there would be a request for my father to play a few tunes on the melodeon. He would go up to the parlour and take it down to the kitchen, where he would play many old tunes. After a while some would take the floor for a half-set. *"Mind the dresser"*, would ring out as a side plate often ran the risk of being dislodged, not to mention my mother's precious crockery mugs doing their own dance from the vibration created by the dancers on the floor.

In our house we had a beautiful *'His Master's Voice'* gramophone, which was played on Sunday evenings only. The favourite record was *'The Rose of Tralee'* and songs of Delia Murphy were also very popular. After a time someone would say, "That's enough of Delia for one night!"

I remember that the used gramophone needles were ideal for one of our pastimes. We would place them in the form of our initials on the railway track and when the train ran over them they became embedded in the steel, as the metal in the needles was much harder than that in the track. It was a great thrill to see your name stamped in the tracks for all time! That same idea was put to use in an attempt to increase our wealth. By putting a halfpenny on the track we hoped that a heavy goods train would flatten it out and make it into penny size. Of course the result was disastrous – the halfpenny was flattened beyond all recognition and had to be thrown away.

# ENGINE WHISTLES.

## ENNISKILLEN STATION.

| | |
|---|---|
| Trains approaching Enniskillen from Sligo Main Line .. .. .. | *Three Long Whistles* |
| Trains for Sligo Company's Dock Platform, No. 1 Line .. .. .. | *One Short Whistle.* |
| From Sligo Company's No. 1 Line to No. 2 Line, and *vice versa* .. .. | *Two Short Whistles.* |
| From Sligo Company's No. 1 Line to Carriage Dock, and *vice versa* .. .. | *One Short Whistle and a Cockcrow.* |
| From Carriage Dock to No. 2 Line, and *vice versa* .. .. .. .. | *One Long and One Short Whistle.* |
| From Sligo Company's No. 1 Line to Exchange Siding, and *vice versa* .. .. | *Three Short Whistles.* |
| From Sligo Company's No. 2 Line to No. 3 Sligo Company's Goods Siding and *vice versa* .. .. .. .. .. .. .. | *Two Short Whistles and Cockcrow.* |
| From No. 2 Sligo Line to Great Northern Company's Cattle Beach, and *vice versa* .. .. .. .. .. .. .. | *Four Short Whistles.* |
| From Exchange Siding to Carriage Dock, and *vice versa* .. .. .. | *Five Short Whistles.* |
| From Sligo Company's No. 1 Line to Great Northern Company's No. 1 Line, and *vice versa* .. .. .. .. .. .. | *Five Long Whistles.* |

## SLIGO STATION.

| | |
|---|---|
| From Ballysodare to Passenger Station, and *vice versa* .. .. .. | *One Whistle.* |
| ,, ,, Goods Station, and *vice versa* .. .. .. | *Three Whistles.* |
| From or to Engine Shed Sidings .. .. .. .. .. .. | *Two Long Whistles.* |
| Backing out of Passenger Station .. .. .. .. .. | *One Long Whistle.* |
| Down to Up Line, and *vice versa* (Station) .. .. .. .. | *One Long and Two Short Whistles.* |
| ,, ,, ,, ,, (Eastern end of Station) .. .. .. | *Two Short Whistles.* |
| From or to No. 1 Siding (Passenger Station) .. .. .. .. | *Three Short and One Long Whistles.* |
| ,, ,, No. 2 Siding (Passenger Station) .. .. .. .. | *Two Short and Two Long Whistles.* |
| ,, ,, Carriage Dock (Passenger Station) .. .. .. .. | *One Short, One Long and One Short Whistle.* |

Page from SL&NCR Service Time table, 2 June 1936

'Lough Melvin' at Castlecoole Woods, Enniskillen 1954. Photo: N. Sprinks

# CHAPTER THREE

# Schooldays

I started school at the age of six in May 1936. Kathleen, Tommy and I walked the one and a half miles in sunshine, hail, rain or snow. Our national school, St. Joseph's, was built in 1910 in the townland of Carrowcrin and was known locally as Sracomer school. There were two classrooms divided by a folding partition whose top half had beautiful, thick corrugated frosted glass. The lower portion was made of stained teak timber.

In my time there were roughly eighty pupils on the roll book. There were three members of the same family teaching in the school, Henry McMorrow, and his sisters Ann and Margaret. Sometimes classes took place in one of the cloakrooms. Teachers were very strict in those days. Henry was a big, tall build of a man. Known locally as 'Big Henry' he was well liked by all who knew him. He lived in Market St., Dromahaire and cycled four miles to school each day. I remember that a step protruded from the axle of the back wheel of his bike. He would put his foot on this step and glide forward onto the saddle. If the weather was extremely bad he used to employ Josie Fowley, a local taxi man, to take him to school.

Henry was fond of using the black sally rod. When he came into the classroom in the morning he had a habit of striking his broad legged trousers with the rod. The swishing sound had the immediate effect of making you sit up straight in your desk. Sometimes the rod met with an accident when the teacher wasn't on the scene! On discovering the broken stick Henry would call up a lad, Jack O Rourke, to the top of the class and hand him a big penknife, which he carried in his trousers pocket.

"Go out there into Michael McMorrow's (no relation of Henry's) field and up along the hedge there, you should find a good black, sally rod and bring it to me", he would say.

This announcement would send a cold shiver down our spines. In fairness he didn't use the rod all that much though some pupils said he was very cross. Maybe it was a blessing on a cold day – at least your hands were always warm!

In November 1939 a new teacher from Waterford city came to work in our school. His name was Eugene Mulhooley and he was a very good teacher indeed. I remember however, that we had some difficulty getting used to his Munster Irish because up to that we were used to the Connaught dialect. Since Irish was my favourite subject at school I found the difference very interesting. Many years after he retired he and his wife Eileen, who was a teacher also, decided to leave Dromahaire and they went to live in the village of Rathmore, Co. Kerry. Sadly, shortly after going there, Eileen died. Eugene is now eighty seven years of age, hale and hearty. I'm glad to say that in over fifty five years I have not lost contact with him. Each year we exchange Christmas cards and I have called to see him a couple of times.

On our way to school we used to pass the Travellers' camp at Buggsturn about three hundred yards from our house. The camp belonged to Tom Ward and his wife and they usually came twice a year to our area with their large family. The tent was of green canvas and inside the beds were made up of layers of straw, which Tom got from some of the farmers in the neighbourhood. Nearby was his spring cart, painted in various colours, with really lovely floral designs. The horses' leather harness was dotted with brass studs. The Wards' other possessions included a bantam cock and hens with rings on their feet; two piebald horses and an undernourished greyhound.

Often, we as children were nervous passing the camp in the morning. Usually there wasn't a sound from the travellers but on some mornings the silence would be broken. Tom's strong voice would be heard echoing through the canvas with questions such as, "What time is it children?

" Ye didn't see the brindle back the road?

" Did ye see the two piebalds abroad in the woods?

" Would any of ye children have a *Wild Woodbine* on you to spare?"

Tom lit the fire in the open and in stormy, wet weather he made hoops of hazel rods and set them in the ground round the fire. Over the hoops he draped a sheet of porous sacking. The sacking had a two fold purpose. It shielded the fire from storm and it also let through the sharp smelling smoke rising from the wood fire. Buggsturn was a good place for a camp. The horses could graze in the plantation and there was plenty of firewood available. Tom's wife and some of their children would call to various farm houses in the area looking for food. My mother used to give them milk and potatoes and sometimes half a soda cake. They were always very thankful for anything they got, be it little or large. I know now that they were forced into begging, for in fact both Tom and his wife were both very industrious and tried to make ends meet by their respective skills. Tom was a tinsmith and was an expert maker of porringers or 'ponnies' as they were called. The cans were well-made, with lids attached and some had beautiful designs punched out on the lids. With his horse and spring cart, Tom would go to Dromahaire village and buy sheets of tin from the hardware shops of S.J. Gilmor and G.J. Robinson. The tin was supplied by Thomas Henshaw and Company, Dublin. It came by rail to Dromahaire station in half ton consignments. The tin sheets measured about 30" by 18".

Often in the evening on our way home from school we stopped at Tom's camp-site to watch him make his various utensils. His main tools were a hammer and a cutters. From the small strips of tin left over he made whistles for us. He cut a piece of tin about two inches and folded a light edge on both sides. He then pushed another small length of tin into the first piece leaving a very small space between them. The whistle sound was very shrill. Apart from porringers, Tom also made small cans and a large milking can known as a half-gallon. His wife made beautiful flowers from crepe paper. The paper was secured on light wire. Carrying bunches of various sizes she went round the houses selling them. My mother would buy some from her and place them in two small vases sitting on a shelf underneath the Sacred Heart picture.

After about a month or so, fodder for the Travellers' horses would begin to get scarce in the Plantation and along the road sides. When Tom noticed this, he would move with his family to some other part of the country. My father was glad to see them go because he worried that the horses, now short of food, would break down the railway fences and wander onto the tracks. For their second visit of the year, which was usually in late spring the Travellers always camped in the same site. People in the area never fully realised how bad their plight was, though it was often said that there were other itinerant families living in worse conditions. In the 30s people were themselves struggling to eke out a living. However, we as children often wondered how the Wards could survive the bitter cold of a heavy night's frost as we headed for school with our sods of turf under our oxters for the school fire.

The sods would be wrapped in *The Leitrim Observer* and tied with twine. It must be said that we only brought turf in this way when the weather was exceptionally severe over a prolonged period of time. The usual school heating arrangements were as follows – each pupil was required to supply one donkey load of turf. This meant two creel fulls. Some 'suppliers' gave the bare amount, others put *crivins* on, meaning the turf was built above the level of the creels. Since there were three of us, my father had to provide three donkey-loads or six creels. I loved bringing the supply to school and I would continually pester my father to allow me to do so. I had to make three journeys with the donkey, which of course took all day! No classwork for me at any rate. Pupils whose parents didn't supply turf gave money instead. This worked out at four shillings per pupil. When all the subscriptions were collected by the teachers, two horse-cart loads of turf were purchased with the money. The man who supplied the turf arrived at the school before lunch-time. He left the load at the roadside because the gate into the yard was too narrow for a cart to enter. At lunch time the pupils carried the turf about fifteen yards to the shed which was situated at the back of the school.

Across the road, opposite our school, lived a grand old lady named Bessie Hannon who wore a beautiful black shawl. Her two-roomed cottage was neat and tidy and on each side of the fireplace were two 'soft' chairs. In the summer months the teachers would get the kettle boiled in Bessie's. Sometimes they sent a couple of eggs to be boiled in the black porringer. One of the pupils would come across to her on this errand. Bessie felt honoured to perform this task for the teachers.

We were always glad to get home from school for 'Níl aon tinteán mar do thinteán féin'! Sometimes we would run up the railway line in the evening to meet the workmen coming home on the bogie. A spin on the bogie was a great thrill. It could travel down the line at speed and because it had no brakes – a navvy shovel pressed on its wheels was the way to bring it to a halt. The bogie was used to carry the workmen's tools and materials to the wooden toolbox at our house, where they were stored for the night. Then the main bogie frame was lifted off and placed alongside the line. The wheels were removed and secured with a chain and lock in case vandals might attempt to put them on the tracks.

One of the most vivid memories of my schooldays was the creaking sound that came from the expanding rails in the intense heat of summer. It usually began around four o'clock after we had come home from school. We could hear the noise through the open doorway while eating our dinner in the kitchen. In the late of the evening, around nine o'clock, as the rails cooled, the noise became louder. When we put an ear close to the rail we could hear the lovely 'running' noise all along the track. During one very hot summer the rails buckled in several places, for a mile or so, between Castledargan and Ballygawley and train services had to be suspended. To offset the risk of buckling, a slight space was left between lengths of rail. The train wheels passing over these spaces produced the clickety-click noise so familiar to travellers of years ago. Nowadays a new method of rail-laying has eliminated the 'clickety-click'. Known as C.W.R. – Continuous Weld Rail, expansion is allowed for by splicing of the rails.

## Trains Stopped by Accident, Failure, or Obstruction.

When a train is stopped by an accident or from any cause (unless it has arrived at or passed the Home Signal) the Guard, if there be only one, or the Rear Guard, if there be more than one, must immediately go back at least three-quarters of a mile (unless he arrives at a Signal-box within that distance) to stop any following train, and in addition to his Hand Signals he must take Detonators (to be used by day as well as by night), which must be placed upon the line on which the stoppage has happened as follows, viz. :—

1 Detonator a quarter of a mile from his train ;
1 Detonator half a mile from his train ; and
3 Detonators, ten yards apart, not less than three-quarters of a mile from his train ;

and must also continue to exhibit his Hand Danger Signal to stop any coming train.

See Rule 217 of General Rule Book.

## RULES FOR GATE-KEEPERS.

1. Unless special authority be given to the contrary, the Gates must always be kept shut across the Public Road, except when required to be opened to allow the line to be crossed.

2. When it is necessary for the line to be crossed, the Gate-keepers must, before opening the Gates, satisfy themselves that no Train is near ; they must then place the Fixed Signals (where provided) at danger, to stop all coming Trains, and such Signals must remain at danger until the line is clear, when the Gates must be closed across the Public Road, and Signals taken off. The Gate towards which Road Vehicles, Cattle, Horses, or other Animals are approaching must not be opened until the opposite Gate has been first opened, so as to allow them to cross over without stopping upon the line.

3. A Hand Signal by means of a Flag by day and a Lamp by night must be given to all Trains by Gate-keepers. Gate-keepers must take particular notice of each Train as it approaches and passes, and if they see anything wrong they must show a Danger Signal to the Engine Driver and Guard, and, if necessary, exhibit Danger Signal where a Signal Post is provided, and place three Detonators on the rail against any following Train or any Train coming in the opposite direction.

4. The Lamps on Level Crossing Gates must, when lighted, show a Red Light in each direction along the line when the Gates are closed across it. The Lamps must be lighted as soon as it commences to be dusk, and in foggy weather or during falling snow, and they must not be put out until after the last Train has passed.

5. Traction or other heavy engines, heavy loads of timber, &c., or droves of animals, must not be allowed to cross the Railway when any Train can be seen or is known to be approaching in either direction. For further instructions as to Traction Engines, see Rule No. 120 in Company's Rule Book.

6. At Level Crossings where Fixed Signals are provided, the Gate-keepers must test their working both by day and by night. Gate-keepers and others in charge of Gates, Signals, or Points, must give notice to the Inspector of Permanent Way, Foreman, Platelayer, Ganger, or other person in charge of repairs, immediately any repairs are required thereto. If any part become defective or broken, or should any Gate not close properly and fasten itself on the instant of its being shut, they must immediately request the nearest Platelayer to have the same put right, and the matter must be reported to the Permanent Way Inspector.

7. A copy of the current Service Time Table must at all times be in the possession of the Gate-keeper, and when it becomes worn out or lost a new one must be applied for.

8. When Special Trains are run a printed or written notice will be sent to the Gangers and Gate-keepers when practicable. A Red or Green Board by day, and an extra Red Tail Lamp at night, carried on the last vehicle of a Train, or on a single Engine, indicates that a Special Train is to follow.

As, however, Special Trains or Engines have frequently to be run without previous notice of any kind, it is necessary at all times to be prepared for such extra Trains or Engines.

Page from SL&NCR Service Time table, 2 June 1936

## CHAPTER FOUR

# Inspection & Maintenance of the Line

As a boy, I remember well the annual inspection train. The coach, on which the inspection group travelled, was beautifully furnished with armchairs. The floor was carpeted and there was glass panelling on the walls. The inspection group included some of the Railway Company directors; George Heuston, the Lodge, Dromahaire; Mr McMullen from Sligo; Harry Wynne, engineer; S.C Little, the General Manager and Inspector P McGinnis.

The train stopped at all the level crossing gate houses. I remember the officials going into our house and looking around. Then they went outside to check that all the signal levers were oiled and clean and that the signal and gate lamps were in good order. Everything was ship-shape for the inspectors, for we would have prior warning of their arrival. So there was plenty of time to have the hedges neatly trimmed, the grass cut out to the verge of the railway track and the walls white-washed. From the late thirties onwards, a less elaborate type of inspection took place. Officials availed of the scheduled services to carry out their work.

A feature of the maintenance of the track was the use of dry coal cinders for ballast renewal, particularly along wet stretches of the railway. The cinders were collected from the locomotive shed at Sligo. There was an agreement between CIE and the SL&NCR that the latter could collect the cinders from the engines using the Midland and Great Southern lines. Up to twenty engines, including the SL&NCR one, per day used the locomotive shed. On an appointed day the SL&NCR placed their empty ballast trucks on a siding, close to the shed and milesmen were picked from their gangs to travel on the early morning railcar to Sligo to load the cinders onto the ballast trucks.

CIE also supplied a man named Pat Mullen to assist at loading. We, as children, used to be delighted when my father was detailed to go to Sligo on this work because he always brought back sticks of pink and white rock called *Peggy's Leg*. We could never understand how the words 'A present from Sligo', were imprinted on the rock.

After the ballast wagons were loaded they were attached to a SL& NCR morning goods train and detached at Collooney station. The ballast train left Collooney on an agreed day, arranged by the Permanent Way Inspector and the station master. On board was a gang of men with navvy shovels. The train travelled slowly along the tracks, unloading the cinders at the required marked places. The same procedure was operated from the Enniskillen direction.

The spreading of the cinders along the track, for some reason, encouraged the growth of dandelions. I remember there was a beautiful yellow carpet of these flowers beside our house. When they went into seed large numbers of goldfinches converged to feed on the seed heads. Every day you could count up to forty of them in clutches. These beautiful birds alas, seem to be declining in numbers now.

For a number of years the SL&NCR used a special train, in the month of July, to poison the weeds along the track. It operated from Enniskillen to Collooney and then on to Carrignagat, near Ballisodare and it consisted of two large rail tankers of weedkiller, a wagon with spraying apparatus, a guard's brake van, hauled by a steam engine. Notice of this train would be given to gatekeepers a few days in advance. They were advised to secure and cover all shrubs and flowers in their gardens and along the railway line. The company accepted no responsibility for any damage done by the weedkiller spray. My parents put canvas and jute covers all along our garden. My mother used to take extra care to protect her flowers and especially the beautifully scented rambling roses, which were in full bloom in July, and were priceless in her eyes. She also kept her flock of hens off the line for a week or so until she considered that the effects of the weedkiller had worn off.

The train moved slowly, spraying its poison. The men operating the sprayers were dressed in special gear and they looked like people from another planet. This special weedkiller train was hired from the GNR. In later years it was discontinued due to the cost of hiring – it was one of the cut backs of the SL&NCR when they found that their financial position was under threat.

The Permanent Way Inspector had overall responsibility for the line's maintenance, while each gang of milesmen – usually consisting of six – was given a length of track to maintain and check. For a stretch of six to eight miles the team would have to maintain fences and bridges, clean drains, check culverts and in regard to the track, check alignment and replace worn sleepers. Rail laying was the toughest and most dangerous task – heavy rail lengths had to be lifted manually and put into place. Milesmen's tools included sledge hammers, short-handled navvy shovels, crow bars, different kinds of saws, steel cutters, hedge knives and scythes. Each gang of men had its own bogie. The milesmen's work was very hard and especially when they had to be on the track in very severe weather.

The Permanent Way Inspector was William McBride from Lurganboy and the milesmen I knew were:

**Collooney to Dromahaire:** John Quinn, Thomas Fowley, Michael Drumm, Jack McGovern, John Conlon, Josie Fallon, James Bredin, Francie Leahy, John Loughlin (who later became Permanent Way Inspector), James Hamilton (my father) Charlie Carty (my uncle), Paddy Fowley, Mickie Carney, Tom Cullen, Michael McDaniel, Michael John Loughlin. **Dromahaire to Manorhamilton:** Tommy Fowley, James McTiernan, Patrick Wynne, Paddy Banks, Owen Rooney, Tommy Parkes, Mick Keegan. **Manorhamilton to Glenfarne:** Pee McKeon, Frank McGowan, Paddy Williamson, James Rooney, Willie Keaney, Michael Clancy, Bernie McMorrow, Jimmy Williamson and Henry Ruddy. **Glenfarne to Belcoo:** Eddie Keaney (Jr) Paddy and John Packenham, Francie Kelly, Eddie Keaney (Sr.) and John Cunningham. **Belcoo to Florencecourt:** Jimmie and Eddie Scott, Pat Mc Aloone, Pat Lunny, John Scales; **Florencecourt to Enniskillen:** Paddy Hegarty, Robert Gault, P. Nolan, John McTernan.

Workmen at the building of J.A. Hosies corn mill, Dromahaire station, 1908

# CHAPTER FIVE

# A Boy Porter in Dromahaire

One evening in October 1945, as my father was passing Dromahaire station on his way home from work, Eddie Lambe, the station master, called to him and explained that there would shortly be a vacancy for a boy porter at the station. Charlie Leahy who was porter in Dromahaire was 'getting on' and he had been informed that he wouldn't be able to cope with all the duties involved. The war was just over and goods traffic had increased a hundred fold at the station.

"If your son Michael would be interested in the job," Eddie said, "just write me a letter saying that you would like to have him considered for the position. I will forward the letter to the General Manager's office in Enniskillen."

When my father arrived home with the news I was "over the moon'. I had visions of myself all dressed up in my uniform – peaked cap with S.L.&N.C.R. in red lettering on its front; blue jacket with plain silvery buttons and dark brown corduroy trousers. I can tell you that at fifteen the uniform was the big attraction for me! A few days after the letter was written, I received notification to travel to Enniskillen on the early morning railcar for an interview and to bring my birth certificate with me. Everything went fine and in two days I was notified that I had got the job and to report to the station master for work on the following Monday morning. That morning I was shown around the station area and my duties were outlined to me. My pay was twenty eight shillings a week. The next day I was approached by John Ward the union secretary to join the National Union of Railway men, (N. U. R.). I became a member and remained one for forty six years.

I soon got to know what work was really all about. It was rough-going in those days – loading goods wagons, shunting goods trains and keeping the platforms, offices and waiting rooms nice and tidy each day. I had to be in attendance for the arrival and departure of all Enniskillen and Sligo trains and railcars to assist with the unloading of mailbags, parcels and newspapers. In the winter months I oiled the standard platform and gate lamps and trimmed their wicks. I also climbed the signals to service the oil lamps. Because there was no electricity at the station, the most dangerous operation in which I took part was shunting in the dark winter nights. Looking back on it now, I realize it was nothing short of madness but there was no alternative in those days. In summer my duties included pumping daily, by hand, one thousand gallons of water from the Bonet river for use in the station and the toilets.

Life at the station was very varied. I remember particularly the postmen who arrived to pick up the mail in the morning. The first collection was at 7.00am and the mail was taken into Dromahaire post office. The postmen I recall were: Mattie Kivlehan, Paddy Scott, Jack Mc Gowan, Paddy Madden and Robbie Armstrong. Robbie, a pipe smoker was great fun. He was getting on in years when I first got to know him and I remember that if he was detailed to collect the mails from the 4.00 p.m. railcar from Sligo, children who travelled home by this railcar used to help him push his handcart into Dromahaire. I thought it was a kind gesture on their part. Paddy Scott wore his cap tilted slightly to the left. On the run up to Christmas he was always well positioned when a half-one of whiskey was being poured out because at that time of the year the postmen got a hot whiskey or tea and currant-bread. As he waited to collect his mails, Paddy was always good for a few songs, his favourite being 'Kate from Ballinamore'. He had a great deep voice and was one of the nicest men you could meet. Jack Mc Gowan was another pipe smoker. He was very correct in checking his mailbags and I clearly remember his beautiful handwriting. Paddy Madden was a very sincere man who always seemed to be in a hurry to collect his bags and get back to the village. Mattie Kivlehan was something else – an out and out comedian, who had a word for everyone. In his early days he used to sell newspapers when the trains arrived. As the train was leaving the station he sometimes had difficulty in finding the change for the customer. Mattie was very quick-witted and on one occasion when a commuter leaned out the train window looking for "tomorrow's paper", Mattie replied, " I'm awful sorry sir, I sold it yesterday".

The postmen were always dressed in full uniform, with a great shine in their brass buttons and their boots well polished. There was a great sense of comradeship between them and the railway men. This was shown whenever the postmaster from Sligo General post office travelled by train to check on the postmen at the various stations. John Divers was the postmaster's name. He wore a blue herringbone jacket and grey trousers and carried his rolled-up black 'mack' under his arm. On boarding the 6.20 a.m. railcar in Sligo he used to go up to the front seat so that he could have a bird's eye view entering the stations. However, word was always telegraphed ahead that "a very special person" was on board!

Apart from the postmen, others to visit the station, though in an 'unofficial' capacity, were the lads of the locality. In the summer time particularly, they used to gather on the platform for the arrival of the last train to see the girls who were coming home on their annual holidays. They looked forward to dances which would be held in the girls' homes, in honour of the homecoming. There were always dances in the house of the McPadden sisters, when they came home on holiday, and the dancing usually went on until six o' clock in the morning with plenty of refreshments.

At other times of the year the local lads used to visit the station and sit in the waiting room. There they mingled with intending passengers for the train and swopped stories and yarns with them. Some of them would be smoking and I remember one lad in particular who knocked the last out of his Woodbine by sticking a straight pin into the butt and smoking it until all that was left was ashes! When the last train was gone and the station was locked up for the night, the lads went over to Ward's shop just across the road. They sat on boxes and bags of meal and céilíed until midnight.

Master John Whyte of Killavoggy cycled down each evening to collect his daily paper. After his purchase he used to cross the road to the station, read his paper for a half hour or so in the waiting room and then light up his pipe before heading for home again.

Among the passengers who used Dromahaire station on a regular basis were children who attended school in Manorhamilton, Sligo and the convent in Ballisodare; nurses employed in St. Columba's hospital, Sligo and farmers and others going to the fairdays in Manorhamilton. A very popular train was the Saturday market train to Sligo. It was usually crowded with shoppers. Master Clancy used to arrive at the station for this train and I had to secure his bicycle for him until his return that evening. The market train was driven by Tommy McTiernan with Paddy Hugh Keaney as fireman, Bernie Gilgunn, relief fireman and Larry Lee, guard. A feature of this train was that the engine ran with its tender first– in other words it travelled in a reverse position from Manorhamilton to Sligo, because there was no engine turn table at Manorhamilton. On a wet, stormy day, this was terrible for the engine crew as they had no protection between the coal tender and their cab, which was open ended.

Also on Saturday, passengers got on at Lisgorman Halt to do their shopping at Dromahaire, where they could spend two hours before catching the return railcar. I remember Johnny Crosswell was one of these Saturday shoppers. We called him 'The Lisgorman Station Master'. Johnny used to dress very well, with waist coat, pocket-watch and chain. He was, indeed, a very jolly man.

I was in my second year in the railway when the big snow of 1947 came. For the two weeks before it fell, the weather was cold and hard with the wind coming from the east. The ground became extremely dry. The snow fell for six hours, from two o' clock in the afternoon until eight in the evening. The Sligo goods train struggled into the station looking like a string of large moving snowballs. It was hauled by the 'Hazelwood' which, although one of the smaller engines, was best suited for the conditions which prevailed. Trans-shipment from its wagons was speedily done to get it on its way to Manorhamilton. As it left the station, we all thought it was an impossible journey to attempt, but the driver and fireman were determined to have a go. Under fierce conditions they battled their way into Manorhamilton but that was the end of the journey. The goods train from Enniskillen had also arrived there and now both were trapped in the same station.

I stayed on duty at Dromahaire station until eight o' clock and I was about to leave when my father, half exhausted, arrived. He had walked a mile, through snowdrifts six feet deep, to ensure that I got home safely.

"What on earth took you here in such conditions?" I asked him.

"Its going to be a tough journey home lad, for both of us," he replied.We set off and half the time we didn't know whether we were on the road or in the fields as everything around us was covered in a blanket of snow. It took us two hours to get to the house.

The railway line was blocked for about two weeks. A large number of staff took part in clearing the snowdrifts off the tracks. Then Tommy Mc Tiernan, and Paddy Hugh Keaney, left Manorhamilton with their engine attached to a large Great Northern Railways van, which had been recovered from the Enniskillen goods train bound for Sligo. The van was fitted with sliding doors. On board were about twenty five railway men armed with broad 'navvy' shovels. The train reached Dromahaire after about two hours. There was great cheering when it came into the station. About twelve others, including myself, went on board and headed for Collooney. We encountered drifts about every quarter of a mile. The train battled on as we cleared each mass of snow and this was the pattern until we arrived in Collooney about three hours later. We were wet, hungry and freezing with the cold. People had gathered to cheer us into the station. After being called together we were told to go into the village for a forty five minute break and refreshments. We adjourned to the nearest pubs– Quigleys, O Connors and Gilhooleys. After a quick 'half-one', a pint or two and sandwiches, it was back to work. The driver and the fireman had taken water on board for the engine and we turned our face homewards. For me it was like a Wild West adventure!

Now that the line was cleared, the goods train from Manorhamilton to

Sligo could run. This was the first train to reach Sligo – trains from Limerick and Dublin were still snow-bound. The clearing of the line brought immediate relief to the local areas. Bread had been in very short supply and there was such a demand from Coyle's Manor - hamilton that this bakery ran out of hampers to carry the bread. The porters in Manorhamilton solved this problem by sweeping clean the floors of the wagons and covering them with brown paper. Then they stacked the hot, baked bread on the paper. On arrival in Dromahaire, I remember the steam from the bread gushing out of the wagons when the doors were opened. It was then conveyed to the country shops by donkeys and creels since no other means of transport could operate in the deep snow. Although most housewives did their own baking, they couldn't get any flour and without doubt the staff of the recently opened Coyle's bakery worked hard to provide a service.

Indeed the snow of 1947 affected the country people least of all because to a great extent they were self-sufficient with their own vegetables, potatoes, milk, poultry, bacon, fruit and oatmeal. For heat and cooking they harvested their own turf from the bog and they could avail of ice-cold spring water from bubbly wells surrounded by water cress.

Sligo, Leitrim and Northern Counties Railway Company.

# Ticket and Contract for the Conveyance of Live Stock

From _Glenfarne_ Station

Route _____

Sender's Name and Address: _Charles Cullen_ _Advarney_ _Glenfarne_

Date _30th May_ 19 _50_

To _Sligo_ Station _____ Railway

Consigneee's Name and Address: _Cook McNeily_ _Sligo_

| Wagon Numbers | Total No. of Wagons | Quantity | Description of Stock | Rate | Paid on | PAID | To Pay |
|---|---|---|---|---|---|---|---|
| | 1 | 1 | Pig | | | 9 - | |
| | | | | | | | |
| | | | 6893 | | | | |
| | | | | | | | |
| | | | Insurance on £ | | | | |
| | | | TOTAL | | | 9 - | |

6.30 am train ex-Sligo on goods siding at Dromahaire station.

# CHAPTER SIX

# The Post-War Years at Dromahaire

Dromahaire station played an important role in the commercial life of the locality in the war years and afterwards. Cattle were loaded in large numbers on the morning trains, destined for Glasgow via Enniskillen and Belfast. The main shippers were James and Mervyn Hamilton and Joe Gorman. Other traffic, via the same route, were consignments of eggs, which were shipped by John Beirne of Drumkeerin to Sinclairs of Glasgow. Three wagons were dispatched each week during the summer months. When loading the eggs into the wagons we had to sort the different cases since there were four brands - 'specials', 'selected', 'standard' and 'pullets'. I remember six of the drivers who brought the eggs by lorry from Drumkeerin – Mick Fee, Eddie Beirne, Hudie McHugh, Eugene McGowan, Michael Davitt and Josie Slevin.

Turf was loaded in Dromahaire and sent via Enniskillen to *Fuel Importers Ltd.*, Barrack Street, Dundalk. Fifty wagons left the station each week, often in 'special' loads. The station was very busy at this time. SL&NCR and CIE lorries took the turf from the bogs of Greaghnafarna, Tullynascreena, Corglancy and Raemore to the station. Leitrim Co. Council workers were responsible for loading the turf into the wagons at the station, since the council had charge of the turf operation during the Emergency, or war years. Pee McMorrow (ganger), Christy Fowley, Denny Keegan, Mick Kemmet, Terence McTernan, John James Hamilton, Pat Conlon and Tom Joe Fowley worked at the loading of the turf. The drivers of the turf lorries were Tom Corcoran and Paddy Conway for CIE and Stephen Murphy, John Roche and Frank Lee for SL&NCR.

In the summer period, eels which had been caught in Lough Gill and surrounding lakes by Co. Fermanagh fishermen, were railed from Dromahaire. Each morning, six large wooden cases of eels, packed in ice and weighing a cwt each, were sent to Billingsgate fishmarket in London.

Inward traffic to the station was quite extensive. Tobacco, cigarettes, snuff, tea, sugar, jams, candles, confectionery, sides of bacon, bales of wrapping paper, twine and paper bags, soaps, boot polish, biscuits were all railed to Dromahaire, as were all items of hardware such as galvanised buckets and baths, bags, horse shoes, horse shoe nails, bales of tin, bundles of hayforks and rakes, hay knives, bags of nails, washboards, creamery cans, scythes, shovels, loys, turf-spades, paints, bicycles and dry wireless batteries.

The traffic in alcoholic drinks and mineral waters was perhaps the largest of all in Dromahaire. Whiskey, beer, cider and minerals arrived regularly, but the greatest trade was in Guinness, large consignments of which were railed daily from Dublin, via Enniskillen, for pubs in Dromahaire, Drumkeerin and Killargue. About eighty firkins of draught Guinness arrived each week and were delivered to the pubs by SL&NCR lorries. The drivers collected all empty firkins and barrels which were sent back to the brewery. Publicans had to record the number on each barrel which was returned. In those days most publicans did their own bottling of stout and beer. Jeiter's Abbey Hotel, in Dromahaire was the largest licensed premises in the area and they bottled two hogsheads a week.

Cement from Drogheda arrived in twelve ton wagons for S.J. Gilmor and O Hara Bros. Dromahaire and also for Frank Dolan, Drumkeerin. Michael Fowley was the carter for Gilmors and Johnny Kelly for O Hara Bros. Large consignments of flour arrived each week from Pollexfen's Flour Mills, Ballisodare. J.A. Hosie, Dromahaire and Frank Dolan, Drumkeerin were the dealers. The Dolan consignments were carted to Drumkeerin, eight miles away, by Felix Cassidy and Frank O Rourke. A ton was loaded on each cart and a cover was securely tied over it. They carted six days a week in all kinds of weather. A set of horse shoes lasted no length, being replaced nearly every week. I knew

Frank and Felix well. Before they set out for Drumkeerin they used to light their pipes and I remember that Felix had a lid on his. In the late spring Frank Dolan's also brought five tons of washing soda and one ton of bluestone for spraying the potatoes. S.J. Gilmor and O Hara Bros. took similar amounts.

The potato crop in those days was vitally important for the household economy and there was intense rivalry among farmers to see who would have the most heaps of potatoes after the digging. A farmer who fell behind in production to a neighbour might cast a doubt on the heaps of his rival by saying - "if the two lairs of rushes and the two foot deep of clay were taken out of the pits, himself and the cat could be in trouble in January next, with supplies running low". Certified seed for the potato and oat crops arrived by rail in early March. Farmers were told at the Sunday masses that the Department of Agriculture inspector, Johnny Benson would attend in McCarrick's Hall, Dromahaire on a particular day to take orders and payments. Later, farmers were notified by postcard to collect the seed at the station. On the appointed day as many as forty carts would arrive. Sometimes, a farmer would leave his consignment in the goods stone, retire to the pub with his friends and forget to come back. Life was easy going that time and there was always 'tomorrow' to collect the seed potatoes.

One of the most thriving business concerns in the area was John Hosie's cornmill, built in 1909 and situated beside the station to which it was linked by a private railway. The Indian corn was railed monthly from Dublin in twelve wagons, each carrying twelve tons. The consignment was made up in twenty-stone bags which were very awkward to handle. Hosie's workmen loaded the bags onto a bogey-type wagon and the corn was pushed into the mill. The bags were then emptied onto a grid and taken by trolly buckets up to the fourth floor from where the corn was fed down on the day of milling. Vera Johnstone and Owen and Jimmy Johnstone worked in the office. Tom McGoldrick, John Devaney, my uncle Tom Carty, Charlie Fowley, Pat McSharry, Pat Timoney and John McSharry worked in the mill. The owner, John Hosie used to cycle to Dromahaire from his home in Castledargan, a distance of six miles, each morning and return on the evening railcar to Ballygawley halt.

During the summer months, on Friday evenings, Paddy Downey of the village post office used to collect from the station a skip or insulated container of Kevinsfort Dairies, Sligo ice cream. The container was brought into the village on the hand cart which also carried the mail. Word used to get around quickly that the ice cream had arrived and within a couple of hours it was sold out. Prices ranged from one penny to sixpence for the various sizes.

On the first day of the month, Station Master Lambe instructed me to collect the accounts from the various shops for goods sent or received by rail. The all-round trip– about twenty five miles– I made by bicycle. In Drumkeerin, John McGrail usually gave me a glass of red lemonade – a real treat in those days . Furey's sweet shop was in the centre of the village and when I called there I always got 'hard sweets' from the big glass jar on the counter. Other shops and pubs, which I remember in Drumkeerin at that time, were Paddy Kellys, McHugh Bros., Frank Dolans, F.C. Dennison, Denis McHughs (who had two pubs), O Rourkes, Rogans,Jack Kellys and Mary Kate Beirnes. Mention of these shops reminds me of the other shops in the rural areas, all now closed forever. It was wonderful to go into one of these country shops and experience the various smells– sides of bacon, tobacco, the tea in open chests and the loose sugar in two cwt. bags. When you went shopping everything was weighed out before your eyes. The bacon was sliced, weighed and wrapped. The paraffin oil was poured into a gallon can. The sweets were weighed and put into a 'thumb-bag' made out of a piece of yesterday's paper. The bar of coarse salt was cut to the amount required. It was likewise with Murrays' Twist tobacco. All the items which had been individually wrapped were given a final wrapping in a sheet of brown paper which was torn from its reel on the counter. The messages were then tied with a length of twine, which dangled from its spool on the ceiling. I remember well the country shops in my area - Pat McGoldrick, John Ward, Mrs. Travers- in the Dromahaire

Station area; John Beirne, Tully (the man who also had a horse-drawn mobile shop); James Latten, Sonny Clinton, Cleen; Michael Keegan, Drumconnor; Hugh Harvey, Little Sweetwood; Harry Bouchier, Cloonagh; Johnny Hamilton, Corglancy; Owen Dolan, Tullycooley; Mattie E. Dolan, Beagh; Michael McSharry, Tullynascreena; John Keegan, Greaghnafarna; Patrick Keaveney, Corritmore; Billie Leith and John McNulty, Killargue and Mary Gallagher, Creevelea.

It was common practice in those years to return empty crates and boxes by rail which meant extra revenue for the railway company. I remember the 'John Players' driver going round to the various shops to collect the empty wooden cigarette boxes. I often helped him to build and sort them on the loading platform. There would be about two hundred cases in all. Other items which were returned included cardboard cartons, jam jars, bottles, hampers, tar barrels, bales of jute bags, sheep and pig crates and whiskey jars.

Another feature of life at Dromahaire station was the arrival and departure of the hackney drivers with their passengers. Among those I remember were Denis McHugh, Denny Keohane from Drumkeerin; Patrick McConnell, Frank Oates, Josie Fowley and Tom O Connor from Dromahaire. Tom, a first cousin of mine, drove for Tess Lee, Drumkeerin. Hugh Harvey from Sweetwood was another hackney man.

# Sligo, Leitrim & Northern Counties Railway Co.

❖

## MEMORANDUM.

FROM GENERAL MANAGER'S OFFICE

ENNISKILLEN.

OUR REFERENCE

To

YOUR REFERENCE

14th April, 19 50

TO ALL CONCERNED.

The Holder, MICHAEL HAMILTON, has permission to travel on
the Company's Rail Cars and trains between Sligo and
Enniskillen and return, to obtain a knowledge of
Guards' duties, etc. on this memo as authority.

S. C. LITTLE

Per

# CHAPTER SEVEN

# Train Guard at Sligo Depot

Towards the end of the 1940s goods traffic at Dromahaire Station was even heavier than when I started work. I found the workload getting intolerable and, although I still enjoyed the atmosphere of the station, I was hoping for a 'green light' to better things. My opportunity came in early 1950 when a rumour went the rounds that a train-guard vacancy would soon arise at Sligo Depot. The rumour proved well founded with the advertising of the vacancy on April 1st. I didn't hesitate but put pen to paper and applied for the job. I addressed the letter to the Traffic Manager, General Manager's Office, Enniskillen.

About a week later I received notification that my application had been successful. Details of my duties were also enclosed and I was to be based at Sligo Depot. I also received a memo, dated 14 April 1950, which authorised me to travel on all railcars, goods and cattle trains in order to familiarise myself with all aspects of the job. After two weeks I began working as train guard on my own, travelling on the 4.00pm railcar to Enniskillen and returning to Sligo on the 7.20pm, passenger and mixed steam train.

I didn't go into digs immediately in Sligo preferring to cycle to work, a round trip of twenty miles, since the weather was beautiful at the time. My rudge bicycle, despite a slight buckle in the backwheel, never let me down. I remember well that the countryside looked extremely well that summer, with every bush and fruit tree in blossom. The omens were good – my wages were now £3-10s-0d a week. My last pay in Dromahaire was £2-15s-0d. Of course there was no 'disturbance allowance' in those days!

The station master in Sligo was John Maloney, who was most helpful to me in every way and indeed all the other staff were always ready to assist me if I needed advice on any matter. I soon became familiar with the layout of the passenger station and of the huge marshalling railway goods yard down at Sligo Quays.

I progressed to a 'week about' system of work – on all the different shifts out of Sligo [i.e 6.20am Rail; 6.30am, Goods and Livestock; 11.45am Goods and 4.00pm Railcar]. I decided to stay in Sligo and took up digs with a grand old lady called Mrs McNiffe. I stayed with her for six years. She packed my lunch each night and called me at 5.00am for the early morning trains. I got my own breakfast. My digs cost £1-10s. per week. Kevin Wilson, a train guard from Manorhamilton also stayed with this kind lady, as did a CIE train driver named Maurice Costello from Dublin, who always worked on a night shift down at Sligo goods depot, working on the 'Pilot Engine'. Shunting of trains went on throughout the night. Maurice's favourite song, which he sang after a few pints, was *'Twenty Men from Dublin Town'*.

When working on the 6.30am goods and livestock train, I used to leave my digs at 5.45am and walk the quarter mile to the passenger station. There I collected my train guard's equipment – shunting pole, oil hand lamp, fog signals and green and red flags. These items were always kept in a place known as the lamp room at the bottom of the passenger platform. Having collected my gear I walked to the goods depot on the Quays– past the signal box and down the branch line to 'take over' my train. It was a lovely walk in the summer months as I listened to the birds singing in the clear morning air. Sometimes I was startled by the sudden dash of a blackbird out of the whitethorn hedgerows on its way to find its early morning breakfast. As I walked further, I noticed on my left a herd of thirty pedigree Friesian cattle owned by the Ursuline Convent. It was a peaceful sight to see the cows lying in the lush, dew-drenched pasture, chewing their cud. Soon the herdsman came to take them to the milking parlour.

Milking started at 6.45am. Three men milked ten cows each, morning and evening. For the early morning milking, they each received one shilling extra. Michael Silke from Galway was the farm charge hand for the Ursuline nuns, who were the first people to introduce the pedigree Friesian cows to Sligo. As I crossed the railway bridge spanning Finisklin road I could see the steam rising from the cattle-loading bank as the over heated animals, who had been driven hurriedly from their overnight sheds a mile away, were being loaded onto the wagons. When loading was complete, these wagons were taken by shunting engine and shunted onto my train. Soon I was ready to go. First I checked that all door pins were secured on each wagon. Then my train climbed out into the beautiful sunshine toward Collooney, where more wagons of cattle were attached to make up a full trainload. Twenty-four laden wagons was the maximum load you could haul on any goods or cattle train under your charge.

As I became familiar with my duties, Harry Taylor, my traffic manager in Enniskillen, would tell me that safety was of prime importance in the working of all trains and his advice was, to be courteous and helpful towards passengers at all times, adding with a half-smile that "the customer is always right".

One of my most most important duties as guard was to ensure that the correct signal was displayed at the rear of my train. This was especially important in the case of goods trains. In the daylight, the train or rail car carried a white tailboard. If a 'special' train was to follow later, it carried a red tail board and if a 'special' was to come in the opposite direction a green tail board was displayed. At night, a train carried a red lamp at its rear, but if a 'special' train was due to pass later, from either direction, two red lamps were hung. These signal arrangements were understood by all gatekeepers and milesmen, along the line, and they took note of the signals as the train went by.

So, as darkness fell, I lit the red tail light and hung it at the rear of my van. Then I lit two white side lamps in the van. These were very important for the driver and fireman. As they looked back the whole length of a long train, the white lights indicated to them that the loose-coupled wagons were intact and that all was well as they sped into the night.

Another of my duties as guard was to deliver the morning newspapers to the various stations. The papers came by road from Dublin and arrived in Collooney by the 'paper' car as it was known. On arrival in Collooney from Sligo I loaded the papers into my guard's van. They were made up in parcels for the various shops along the route:– W Conboy in Ballintogher, PA Downey and JC Ward, Dromahaire; Leonards and Lynotts, Manorhamilton; John Clancy, Glenfarne; JD McGriskan and JB Lennon, Kiltyclogher (unloaded at Glenfarne); Charles Dolan, Blacklion and James Conway, Belcoo.

Between Collooney and Dromahaire I took a copy of *The Irish Independent* out of JC Ward's consignment and when approaching my father's house, I leaned out of the van and threw it right on the door step. My father was probably the first man in North Leitrim to have his morning newspaper on the breakfast table at 7.40am, my scheduled time for passing the house. Each morning the Customs and Excise officer at Glenfarne got complimentary copies of both the *Irish Independent* and the *Irish Press*. They were neatly parcelled in John Clancy's consignment with the word 'complimentary' stamped in red ink on each copy. The officers of HM customs Belcoo also got their complimentary papers in James Conway's batch. The daily newspapers in the early 1950s were $1^1/_2$d each.

At the end of the week, I paid for the week's newspapers in JC Ward's shop. In those days very few papers were bought in the country areas. Sometimes the paper would be passed around from house to house in the townland. However, there was more of a demand if a murder trial was taking place in Dublin.

The author Michael Hamilton in guard's van at Sligo

"Lough Erne" on Weirs Bridge, Enniskillen 1954. Photo: N. Sprinks

# CHAPTER EIGHT

# The Stations

"Lurganboy" at Enniskillen Station.

## ENNISKILLEN

The SL&NCR and GNR merged in Enniskillen and both companies had huge marshalling yards for shunting operations. Enniskillen was the main transfer point for livestock from the west of Ireland. The Ulster Farmers Mart took place on Thursday and so, on Wednesday and Thursday mornings, special SL&NCR trains of cattle arrived for the mart. After being put in large pens the cattle's ears were punched to prove they had entered Northern Ireland legally. Some of these cattle were sent to Omagh, Pomeroy, Dromore and other places. Cattle destined for export via Derry and Belfast were punched at the port of entry.

Among the cattle dealers who sold at Enniskillen mart were the McManuses, Blacklion; the Adamses, Enniskillen; Myles Sweeney, Eugene McNulty and Josh Golden, Manorhamilton; Gerry, Brendan and Paddy Joe Mannion and Des Lang, Collooney; Albert McKenna and Patsy Noone, Sligo. Drovers, who took the cattle to the mart, were Tommy and Dessie Shannon and Dick Currothers. The old mart is now demolished (Dunnes Stores stands on the site) and a new one is located outside the town.

For the safe operation of the large number of trains operating in Enniskillen, two signal boxes were required – a southside box and a northside one. Each day trains arrived from Derry, Belfast, Sligo and Dublin. In the summer time especially, large numbers of Scottish tourists transferred to the Sligo line. The Bundoran express trains were also very busy carrying pilgrims for Lough Derg.

Some of Enniskillen SL&NCR staff I knew were : General Manager: Sam Little; Ernie Monaghan, Accountant; Clerks: Louis Algeo, Edith Monaghan, Jack Bell, Willie Trotter, Samuel Fiddes, Eileen Woods, Robin and Richie Gault. Traffic Manager: Harry Taylor; Shunter/ Guard: Jimmie McHugh, Foreman: John Blair; Yard Staff: Willie Gault, Tommy Harte, John Howe, John Murray; Train Drivers: Paddy Nevin, Paddy McTernan, Tommy McGalloway; Fireman: Michael Harte.

G. N.R. Staff: Station Master: George Agnew; Loco Foreman, Billy Boland; Guards: Harry Gray, George Ramsey, Bertie Keyes; Foreman: Jack McQuaid; Shunters: Vincent Beatty, Dick Currothers, Porters: Tommy Steele, Freddie Cahill, Bertie Lambert; Signalmen: Tommy White, Patsy Rooney, Tommy Callaghan.

'Big Tom' Forde, as he was known, worked on the railway as a miles-man at Enniskillen and although he had retired he still kept a beauti-ful garden of vegetables, just down below the signal box up on the rail-way embankment. On his way down to the garden each evening, he would call into the signal box for a chat, light his pipe and have some tea. One particular evening he called in as usual and told the signal man that he was going down to pick two nice vegetable marrows for the station master as promised.

In the meantime a few of us had come in to make some tea and it was decided to play a trick on Tom. The plan was to wrap two pieces of coal, about the same size and weight as the marrows, in newspaper and exchange them for the station master's marrows. After a while Tom came stepping down the line and was invited up for tea, as usual. He couldn't resist the invitation and left his bag, containing the marrows down beside the coal store – perfect for the exchange. By the time he had finished his tea the signal man had made the quick exchange and Tom headed off again. The atmosphere was tense while we waited to see what would happen. After about five minutes Tom appeared down the platform. He looked in a hurry! Fellows scattered in all directions, except of course for the signal man who had to remain at his post. Tom came up the stairs in a rage and enquired who was tampering with his bag. The signal man sung dumb – nobody knew anything! Tricks were the order of the day, at every opportunity.

Big dairy farmers, who kept herds of Friesian cows, in the greater Belfast area, and who supplied milk to the big dairies around the city, in the harvest time of the year 'culled' and sold off the older beasts in the herd. A cattle buyer for the Castlebar meat factory bought some of the animals, which were then railed, via Enniskillen, to Collooney. I remember on occasions, eight wagons of cows coming in on the Belfast evening train and then being attached to the 7.20pm Sligo train. At Collooney the cattle were transferred to CIE lorries and trailers and transported to Castlebar. They were beautiful animals, in the best of condition. They were so big you could only fit ten cows in each wagon and their backs were almost touching the roof.

A feature of Enniskillen station was the pigeon racing which was popular between July and September. Large crates of these birds arrived at the station from Belfast. The pigeons were released from the platform by Bertie Lambert who was known as the 'pigeon-fancier'. It was a beautiful sight to see hundreds of these birds soaring into the sky to begin their journey home.

Florencecourt Station House 1993.

## ABOHILL HALT & FLORENCECOURT STATION

Abohill was a halt where railcars stopped on request to pick up or set down passengers. When Belcoo had their Annual Sports Day on the 15th August, as many as thirty or forty people used to travel on the 1.45pm railcar ex-Enniskillen and return on the 4.00pm car. Pat Lunny, a milesman in the Abohill area, played the big drum in the Mullaghdun fife and drum band.

Florencecourt station was quiet, dealing mostly in tar for Fermanagh Co. Council. In the early years of the railway sheep farmers sent their wool from here to Foxford Woollen Mills in Mayo. The station master was Archie Burns and the signalman/porter was Michael McCutchen.

# BELCOO STATION

Belcoo was a pretty station, all the buildings being of cut stone. There was a station house, signal box, goods store and another structure which housed a huge water tank on top. It stored thousands of gallons of water for the steam engines. Water for this tank was pumped from a pump house down at the border bridge, which spanned the river Mac Nean three quarters of a mile away from the station. This structure is still there today, without its water tank. It is gratifying to see that the station is still beautifully preserved by its present owner, Mairéad O Dolan. Restoration of the signal box was completed in 1994.

I remember some passengers very well – Johnny McGourty was a cattle buyer for the McManuses of Blacklion and it was said that Johnnie was one of the best judges of a beast in the North West.

I also remember Hughie McKiernan travelling with me in the guard's van to Enniskillen. He always liked to go shopping there. He wore a black bowler hat and carried a walking stick as he was getting on a bit and his eyesight was failing. Once Hughie was seated in the guard's seat he would sing non-stop, all the way to Enniskillen.

In the early 1930s, one of the most unusual traffic items which came to Belcoo station, was wagon loads of live turkeys. Poultry dealers who came from Ballaghaderreen, Co Roscommon, named Mickey Casey, P. Rogan and J. Kilfoyle would buy thousands of turkeys in the North-West for export to Scotland. They attended all turkey markets in the month of November and December and then railed them live to Belcoo station, where they were taken into the large goods store. There they were killed and plucked and made ready for final shipment to Scotland, via Enniskillen and Belfast. Scores of people were employed for this seasonal work. They were paid 3d. for plucking a hen and 4d. for a cock. It was ready money for Christmas as work was very scarce in those days.

Michael Scott, whose father Jimmy and uncle Eddie were employed on SL&NCR, remembers in the 1930s when horses and carts from Dowra

Belcoo Station. Photo: N. Sprinks

and Glangevlin collected meal, flour, paraffin oil, tea and sugar and brought them back to shops along the way. He also remembers that Blacklion creamery brought the cream from the creamery on a 'dray' to Belcoo station for dispatch to the larger creamery of Enniskillen.

The station at Belcoo was officially known as Belcoo and Blacklion Station and was, at the time, apparently unique in Europe because it served two different land boundaries i.e Northern Ireland and the Republic of Ireland. Another unusual feature was that the station master also ran the local post office. On the run up to Christmas the mails were very heavy, coming in from border areas like Tullyrosmearn, Scribbagh and Garrison. I often loaded over fifty bags at Belcoo onto the 4.00pm railcar ex Sligo to Enniskillen, bound for Belfast. If you were smuggling a wee parcel for someone it was very easy to post it here. You just walked across to the opposite platform to the post office, making sure that the customs officer didn't see you. To do this it was necessary to keep him busy, checking customs clearance papers while you made your dash across!

Freddie Monaghan was the station master; signalmen/porters: Paddy McHugh and Willie Wallace; later Willie worked as guard out of Enniskillen. Customs Officers: Gerry Rasdale, William Fletcher, A. J. Brady, James Elliott and John Regan. Their office was on the station platform, for clearance of goods but also to check passengers' luggage. Luggage had to be presented at a long table for inspection. Usually I found all this checking a nuisance, as it often caused unnecessary delays to the schedule.

## GLENFARNE

Glenfarne was busy for both goods and passengers. It was the rail head for Kiltyclogher, some six miles away, and in later years became the rail head for goods traffic for Blacklion and surrounding area. In early summer Leitrim Co. Council got large consignments of tar for road surfacing. Guinness came for Blacklion, Kiltyclogher and Glenfarne. Alex Maguire had a large, wholesale bottling company in Kiltyclogher and his weekly order also came. Paddy Denning was the station master and Pat Clancy the signalman/porter. Customs and Excise had their own office beside the platform and I knew many customs officers – Tom Walsh (chief officer), Tony Gaughan, Michael Tremble, Eamonn Leahy, Michael Scully and Ted O'Keefe. Hugh Gilgunn was the taximan. Postmen were Packie Keaveney, John McGloin and Michael Keaney. Peter McHugh had the contract for bringing of mail to and collecting mail from Kiltyclogher, which he did with pony and cart.

From an engineering point of view Glenfarne Station was not well sited, for either the safe arrival or departure of heavy goods or cattle trains. Most train drivers dreaded taking these trains down into the station, from the Sligo direction, because of the long, steep fall all the way down into Glenfarne station. If the driver hadn't full control, then the final descent could prove to be a nightmare. Over running the station platform was not looked on too kindly by the customs officers, especially.

I remember, as a guard on a heavy goods train, a wagon-coupling snapping just as the train came to the crest of the hill, before we made our descent. I suffered a few anxious minutes until I got the attention of the driver. He, seeing the danger, slowly eased away from the breakaway section, easing the impact when the two sections of the train came together again, thus averting a nasty situation. On the other hand, there was a short steep incline into the station from the Enniskillen side, and this was nearly as bad, as often when pulling very heavy loads, a coupling would break and the broken section would run back (only partly checked by the brake in the guard's van) as far as the Leitrim/Cavan border, three quarters of a mile away!

J. A Hosie had his own flour and meal store built beside the station and wagon loads of flour and meal could be shunted alongside for unloading into the store. He had a miniature railway and bogie ( a miniature flat wagon) in the store. The flour and meal were loaded onto the bogie and then pushed by hand the length of the store, which was quite long. The rails and bogie are to be seen to this day in the store. When J.A. Hosie applied for planning permission to build this store, with residence attached, one of the conditions laid down was that the stone work of the buildings would be similar to that of the station buildings. Michael Keaney is the present owner of the store and lives in the house attached.

## MANORHAMILTON

Manorhamilton station was really the nerve centre of the railway. Here is where the largest work force was employed. There were large carpenters' shops where all cattle and goods wagons were repaired and most of the cattle wagons were built here also. Men who worked there were: Pat Wilson, Johnnie Thompson, Jack McGoey, Gerard and Paddy Wilson, John and Mick Gaffney, Jimmie Mooney, Tommy and Jimmie McGourty, Jimmie Rooney, George Flynn, (carpenter), Joey Darcy, Jimmie McTernan and Charlie Canning (painters). In the blacksmiths shop, were Pat Keaney and Tommy Kelly. In the Loco overhauls, and repair shop were Willie Gray, Gerry Lambe, Paddy Martin, Vickie Holland, Paddy O'Rourke, George Gray, Brendan Rooney, G. F. Egan, Engineer and his office staff Kevin Maher, Dennis McGuinness, Sean McPolin and Dominic Connolly. Train examiners were John Paddy Rooney and Joe McTernan; train drivers were Tommy McTernan, Paddy Hugh Keaney; fireman Bernie Gilgunn. Jimmie Packenham was in charge of the store, issuing all kinds of material and oil products. Jack Mc Gee was the station master and office staff were: Maureen Rooney and Michael Walsh Jr. Porters and guards were: Larry Lee, James McQuaid, Benny Keaney and John Ward, general foreman. Pauric McKeon, Seamus McTernan, Robbie Corscadden, Walter O'Malley, Larry McTernan were signalmen/porters. Road garage staff: Peter Gilmurray, Sean Loughlin, Tom McGourty, Patrick Loughlin. (Mechanics)

Road supervisor: Michael Walshe; bus/lorry drivers: Francie Lee, John Roche, Stephen Murphy, Mick McDaniel, Patrick Loughlin, Terence McTernan, Kevin McGovern. Bus drivers and conductors, who worked on buses from Blacklion, were Leo Rooney, Joe Maguire, Herbert Smith, John Joe Gilgunn, Jimmie Cullen, Jimmie McGovern,

Manorhamilton Station looking towards Enniskillen 1954. Photo: N. Sprinks

Robert Farlow and, let me not forget, Owen Rooney, a 'jack of all trades'.

When Owen wasn't engaged on the permanent way section he would do all sorts of work at the station. In all awkward situations, Owen was 'yer man'. Often, he might be let into the signal box to do duty there. Before Owen would engage in any shunting operations he would warn the train drivers and shunters of the 'golden rules', as he knew them. In nightly shunting he would say to them ... "white is right, red is wrong, and green is gently come along." Another of Owen's sayings, from the signal box to driver, was 'don't go up there too close to those catch points, in case you'd dribble off the rails'.

Postmen included John Daly, John Lee, Willie Duggan, Paddy McSharry and Paddy Rooney. Taximen who took passengers to and from the trains were Jimmy Cullen, Alex McGovern, Michael Skeffington and John McEnroy. Regular carters from the station were Ernie Moore and Willie Somers, who were household names around the town.

Manorhamilton Station looking towards Dromahaire 1953. Photo: N. Sprinks

Customs and Excise had their own office on the platform beside the station master's office for clearance of all cross border goods and live-stock. Officers I knew there were: John Donnellan, Brendan McMahon, John McGinley and Dan O'Hara. Generally customs men were helpful and easy to deal with. Working on the goods train there was a 'mountain' of documents to present to the officers for clearance, and if, at any time, there were any discrepancies, generally the customs officials would help resolve the problem. At times the clearance of goods trains could be a real headache. On the rail cars customs clearance was much faster. One of my many duties was to instruct passengers to have all luggage ready for inspection at Glenfarne and Belcoo.

Occasionally, in late October, six or eight wagon-loads of cows were loaded in Manorhamilton, destined for Roscrea meat factory. They would arrive on foot at the station, cold and very tired, from a 'northerly direction'. Some were 'mad out of their of skins' and were known locally as 'the jumpers' – that, you can figure out for yourself.

A lot of precious time was lost during loading – it was nearly impossible to get them on to the wagons, due to poor lighting at the station and the fatigue of the animals. As I would have to transfer the eight wagons of cows onto the Sligo to Dublin (North Wall) train at Ballisodare, I would phone ahead to tell them. On arrival at Ballisodare the wagons were attached to the goods train, to be brought to Liffey Junction station outside Dublin. Mick O'Connell was the guard on the train at the time. I would meet him down along his train and he would ask, "What's your transfer for tonight?"

"Eight wagon loads of cows for Liffey Junction", I would reply.

When he heard this, the cursing and swearing would start.

"Are they on their feet?"

"Yes Mick", I would reply, "they're standing on all fours!"

"Ah , what else would you say. I'm in for a rough night of it, with those bloody cows." .

Often on occasions when I'd meet him he'd say, "I hope you've no black cows on board tonight" – or words to that effect!

When I think of Manorhamilton, many funny moments come back to me. One such incident happened on a Thursday morning. Myles Sweeney was loading six wagons of cattle for the Ulster Farmers Mart in Enniskillen and in the course of loading he asked Pauric McKeon and Walter O'Malley to 'scissors mark' his cattle. When the loading was complete the two were standing around, still holding the scissors, when they happened to notice that Ernie Moore was waiting to collect the usual morning newspapers from the back of the guard's van. I told Ernie I would get the van pulled up to the platform so that he could unload his papers on to his cart. Ernie kept a brindle greyhound which always came with him to the station. The two lads spotted Ernie's greyhound, lying under one of the seats in the waiting room, so they decided they would give him a nice hair cut. They caught him, got to work, and disappeared. What a sight when Ernie saw the poor dog's two ears. He was 'fit to be tied", and went off looking for the culprits. He was on a loser though. All had vanished for their own good for Ernie always carried a good ash plant with him!

Owen Rooney, as well as being a milesman was also a great handyman and was well able to get himself into and out of awkward situations. During a heavy night's frost, the outside water tap became frozen at G.F. Egan's private house, which overlooked the station. Mrs Egan sent down word for some of the workmen to come up to the house to have the tap thawed out, so Owen was called upon to go there. He set off with his blow lamp and proceeded to work on the tap and the lead piping. After a while the piping "turned over like a swan's neck", according to Owen, and realising he had done more damage than the frost, he quickly left the scene. Enquiries began to take place to establish who had caused such havoc but they didn't yield much. Later in the morning Mr Egan was walking down the platform where he happened to meet Owen. He asked him if he had been up at the tap.

"Ah no Sir!", says Owen, "but I met Jack McGoey coming down that direction with a blow lamp under his arm."

Once more Owen survived one of the many awkward situations he found himself in.

On a bad day you could take your top coat up to the signal box to dry it at the big roaring fire. One day you might get your coat dried handy enough, depending on who was sitting around. On other occasions you would come up to collect your coat only to find that the mouth of the two sleeves had been sewn! Another fellow would dash up the stairs in a hurry and make a grab to collect his coat, only to find it stuck to the wall with a six inch nail. One good pull meant leaving part of the collar of the coat hanging on the wall!

Imagine grown men playing 'Blind Man's Buff'! The Railway version of this game was a great pastime among the many men employed in the wagon building and repair workshops, during the lunch hour. The idea was to draw a ten foot circle on the ground. Participants were then blindfolded, handed a pick-axe and, getting five chances, told to mark a 'strike'. The person hitting the spot nearest to the centre of the circle was deemed the winner. On this particular Monday morning Jimmie Mooney arrived to work wearing his good Sunday cap. At lunch, he threw the cap on the ground beside him and took

SL&NCR Road Bus. Reg. No. EI5040

part. After his third strike he enquired of the lads if he was anywhere near the centre. 'No', was the reply. On the fifth and final try one of the 'bright' fellows lifted Jimmie's cap off the ground and threw it into the circle. When Jimmie's fifth blow hit the ground the pick-axe plunged straight into his own cap. An unlucky strike!

One of the most celebrated incidents associated with Manorhamilton was the case of the missing bus. On a Sunday in the month of September 1948 a bus was hired to take a football team, and its supporters from Blacklion to the 'Bee Park' in Manorhamilton, where they were to take part in a match. The bus left Blacklion, crewed by Joe Maguire (driver) and Jimmy McGovern (conductor), picking up passengers at various points along the way. On arrival in Manorhamilton the bus was parked and left secure while the bus men went for refreshments. This, unfortunately was mostly in liquid form and as the evening wore on they both became separated. Joe, the driver met a man called John Regan, who was always about town. The two visited various pubs and were last seen leaving Paddy Campbell's public house and heading in the direction in which the bus had been parked. Jimmy, the conductor was at this stage gone down as a 'missing person'!

Joe got into his cab and John Regan stepped in through the rear side door. John gave Joe a ring of the bell and off went Joe in the direction of Blacklion. Unfortunately things started to go terribly wrong at this point. About a mile and a half from the town Joe took a wrong turn left onto a narrow road and headed towards Ballyboy mountain. Knowing now that he couldn't get the bus turned he decided to keep going and hope for the best. But that wasn't to be. On the climb up the mountain side he suddenly went in on the grass verge and got stuck. Joe went to get help from Pat McGoldrick, who had a big, blue tractor but his efforts failed and there the bus lay for the night!

Once again the following morning the bus was required to work and the fun started when it became known that it was missing. The supervisor in Manorhamilton was contacted and, in the course of enquiry, was told that 'a big, bright object' had been spotted glistening in the sun on top of Ballyboy mountain. Mr Egan was contacted and the story relayed to him. He immediately took his binoculars down to the station, from where he had a full view of Ballyboy and the missing bus. It took a breakdown crew the whole day to recover the bus and Joe spent the rest of his time with the company as conductor!

Large consignments of goods came from Belfast daily, en route to Sligo, and provided all the necessary customs papers were in order and duty payment cheques attached, the goods were cleared immediately. However in the case of wagons of whiskey, which came in huge wooden barrels, the wagons would have to be detached from the train and placed in the 'Bond Store'. They were placed there overnight (the track ran right through this store) and the store was then locked and secured by two huge sliding doors at each end.

The following morning the customs officer and his assistant would go to the Bond Store to have the whiskey examined as was the procedure. Whiskey was extracted from each huge barrel and tested for its proof or strength. The rate of payment of duty was based on the strength.

Since this 'tested' whiskey, amounting to about a pint or so, could not be returned to the barrel it 'went on the market'. Dan O'Hara, the assistant, would give the lads a nod and immediately, they would hurry down to the 'green van', which stored goods and returned empties. If a suitable bottle couldn't be found, a crate of jam jars was used. Each man put his jar under his coat and headed for the Bond Store. A recognised knock was given and after a while Dan would appear with some of this very strong whiskey and each was rationed out his share. It was so strong it had to be well diluted with water. This was an 'exciting brew' and went down well but the day's work had also to be scaled down! Many came so badly 'under the weather' they wished they had never gone near the Bond Store, describing the whiskey being poured into the jam jar "like syrup".

## DROMAHAIRE

Dromahaire had the only two-storey station house on the line. The ground floor comprised the general office, waiting room, ladies toilet and also the station master's living room and kitchen. Upstairs were the family bedrooms. Water for the station toilets was pumped from the Bonet river about two hundred yards away. The station master was Eddie Lambe and the porter was Tom McQuaid and before him Charlie Leahy.

## BALLINTOGHER

Ballintogher Station wasn't very big and had no rail sidings where wagons could be detached from goods trains; all its goods were transhipped from the wagons onto the platform. The same applied to Guinness consignments for the local village pubs. A lot of school children travelled on the railcars from here to schools in Ballisodare and Sligo. Paddy Farmer was the man in charge of the station. The postman was Stephen Byrne and he would take mails to and from the trains.

Train drivers on Sligo bound mixed steam trains didn't like the idea of having to stop their trains here, as there was a very steep incline out of the station and a wet and windy night could present a problem, causing the train to lose time.

Sligo bound trains had to run on schedule, if possible, otherwise when they got to the Collooney/ Ballisodare section the outer home signal would show red, indicating that the Dublin passenger train had been given first preference. If this happened then there was a further delay, as the Enniskillen train could not enter the Ballisodare station until the Dublin or Limerick one had left! In fairness, if the signal man thought you wouldn't block CIE trains, he would take you into the section and give clearance; this is what safe railway working was all about.

## COLLOONEY

Where cattle shipments were concerned, Collooney was the all important centre. Cattle from all over the west of Ireland were loaded at the station. Harvest time was the peak time for such shipments and I remember as many as five 'specials' would leave daily from here, often running throughout the night. It was this traffic that the company really depended on for survival. Each train would have twenty to twenty four wagons and each wagon held twelve to fourteen cattle, depending on size. Often on a Sunday night, cattle dealers would 'light load' twenty wagons – say eight cattle to each wagon – and water and feed them. Early in the morning loading would be completed or 'full loaded'. This helped speed up departure of the first train and kept traffic flowing on time.

Cattle dealers shipping from here were: John McGarry, Hugh Mullen, Cosgrove & Clarke, Felix Bourke, Ned Sharkey, Roy Buchanan, Patsy Noone, Patrick McGarrigle, Hugh Strain, Mulbery Hamilton, Packie O'Reilly, Eamonn Foley, G McDermott. Others sending to the Ulster Farmers Mart were, Dessie Lang, Paddy Joe, Gerry and Brendan Mannion, Collooney; Albert McKenna Sligo; Adams, Enniskillen, Patrick Durkin, Swinford; McManus Brothers, Blacklion.

Goods train ex Sligo leaving Collooney hauled by engine 'Sligo.'

John Corrigan and John and Michael Taheny kept cattle overnight for many of these dealers. They watered and fed them and loaded them at the station the following morning. They had huge sheds, adjacent to the station, to house those cattle. I remember, on each cattle train there was an 'ambulance' wagon. In fact, what it really meant was that it was empty! It was used in the event of cattle 'going down' in wagons or for those getting bruises or injuries. It was, therefore, essential, but was often abused by cattle dealers. For example, a dealer could arrive with forty five cattle for Glasgow and insist on booking them into three wagons, knowing full well that only thirteen cattle per wagon could ride safely. Rather than hassle with him, especially if he was a good customer, six of the forty five would be loaded into the 'ambulance wagon', thus taking unfair advantage of this facility and creating problems if injured cattle had later to be loaded onto it en route.

Staff at the station were: Signal man/Porter: Amby Devaney and Marty Mannion; Station Master: Paddy Denning (Sen.); Office Clerk:

Mary Denning; Company Rep, Frank Denning, who attended most fairs in the west of Ireland canvassing dealers to send their cattle on the SL&NCR route. I remember Paddy Hennessy calling at the station each day. He used to collect the Passionist priests from the Graan in Enniskillen and take them to the Cloonamahon monastery outside Collooney. They were regular travellers on the train. Wilber Middleton who had Corn Mills in Collooney got his Indian Corn from Sligo on the SL&NCR train from the 1930s to '47. Gillhooley's shop got their coal and fertilizer, because the SL&NCR rate was much cheaper than that of the MGW (Midlands Great Western) railway, which these customers could have used.

## BALLISODARE

Leaving Collooney and at Carricknagat the SL&NCR line ran along the CIE main line all the way into Ballisodare station, where it switched onto the CIE main running line. As SL&NCR had the running rights over their lines from here to Sligo it was double line working – all trains using the 'down' line into Sligo and all trains leaving Sligo using the 'up' line.

Working over double lines, one had to become familiar with the workings, rules and regulations set down, as they were somewhat different to those set down for single line working. Occasionally the CIE Rail Inspector, Andy Keogh would examine us on our knowledge. For example, in the event of an accident, 'wrong line' workings might have to be applied and, from a safety point of view, as a guard it was necessary to know how it worked.

Ballisodare was quite busy– Pollexfen's Flour Mills was the railway's best customer. The railway went down to the mill and they had large sidings for placing wagons of grain. SL&NCR carried the bulk grain wagons from Navan and CIE also carried large numbers of wagons from all over Ireland. SL&NCR collected wagons of flour for all parts of Donegal, for J.A. Hosie at Dromahaire and his stores at Manorhamilton and Glenfarne and for Francis Dolan (Wholesaler) Drumkeerin. SL&NCR also carried the wagons of silver ore for Belfast, for shipment to Scotland from the Abbey Mines at Ballisodare.

All wagons of goods and livestock were transferred at Ballisodare for destinations on the midland line and all goods and livestock were transferred at Sligo Quay for destinations on the Great Southern Railway.

Staff I knew were: Vincent O'Shea, Gerry O'Connor, Matt Shanley, Paddy Newman, Michael Cosgrove and Paddy O'Grady. Michael Morrison was the station master. This station is now closed to all goods and passenger traffic. This is indeed sad, for I remember it being a very busy place.

## SLIGO STATION

At 5.00am every morning, cattle loading began at Sligo station. Porters Paddy Ward and Mick Duck assisted in the loading of the cattle. Insulated containers of chilled meat were also loaded from the Cosgrave and Clarke meat factory, at the point where the docks railway line ran alongside the factory. Eight containers of meat where loaded during the night, which ensured that the first goods and livestock train was ready to leave Sligo Quay at 6.30am for Enniskillen. Twelve wagons of cattle, eight wagons of meat and four wagons of eggs comprised this train. Since there was a very steep incline from the goods depot at the quays, all heavily loaded trains had to be 'banked'. 'Banking' meant that a shunting engine was positioned at the rear of the train to assist the train to haul the wagons for a mile or so.

One of the great sources of revenue for the SL&NCR was income from the carriage of large consignments of Guinness to Sligo. The GNR canvassed this traffic and they transferred the wagons of Guinness to the SL&NCR at Enniskillen. The large wholesale bottlers in Sligo– Higgins & Keighrons, Foley & Co., O'Connor Bros., John Egan & Son – all received stout for bottling. The hogsheads were delivered from the station by horse and dray and draught stout was also supplied to the pubs in the town. About eight wagons of Guinness arrived each day at the goods station on the quays, and at Christmas, special Guinness trains were put into operation.

In 1946, Guinness decided to build a specially designed depot so that the draught stout could be 'conditioned'. Each daily consignment was stored for a week before delivery. Consequently the delivery service in the North West greatly improved.

The store had a very low ceiling which conserved the heat coming from the special heating radiators. It was built on CIE property with a rail siding along it and wagons could now be easily unloaded. When this facility was in place, GNR and SL&NCR lost the Guinness business to CIE. All that the SL&NCR retained was the haulage of this traffic locally –to Ballintogher, Dromahaire, Manorhamilton and Glenfarne railheads.

The goods traffic out of Sligo was large and varied. I remember on one occasion a hundred tons of tea coming by boat into Sligo dock, destined for warehouses in Belfast and for the Sligo tea merchants, Benson, Pass and Slater. It took twenty wagons to take this consignment by rail to Enniskillen, where it was transferred to the GNR for final delivery to Belfast. On another occasion, when I came on duty for the 6.30am goods and livestock train, the shunter greeted me with, "You'll not be stuck for an egg this morning". When I went down I found seventeen wagons of eggs attached to the train. The eggs had been delivered the night before from Claremorris, on the Limerick goods train and were destined for Sinclairs in Glasgow.

When the ESB was building the peat powered station in Gweedore in Donegal, the machinery required was shipped into Limerick port and was brought by rail to Donegal, via Sligo, Enniskillen and Strabane. Well over a hundred wagons of machinery was carried by SL&NCR from Sligo to Enniskillen over a period of time. Among the other goods carried on the line were seed potatoes and oats from Donegal for the western counties, beet from Monaghan and Donegal for Tuam sugar factory, timber and coal from Belfast and salt from Carrickfergus.

SL&NCR train crews who worked on trains in and out of Sligo were: train drivers: Joe Lambe, Tommy Masterson, Paddy Meehan, Jimmy Keaney, Jack Connolly, Joe Dunbar, Mick Kearins, Tommy Marren,

Gerry O'Connor, Johnny Hegarty; firemen: Bertie Hegarty, Joe Neilan, Jimmy Roberts, Tommy Hamilton (my uncle), Brian Melly, Paddy Condron; steam fire raisers: Mick Kearins (Jr.) and Louis Kearins; train guards: Dick Patterson, Paddy McLoughlin, Tommy and John Mannion, Martin Brannigan, Dick Rooney, Kevin Wilson, Jack Parkes and my good self.

CIE staff I knew were:  station master: John Maloney; rail passenger foremen: Con Hegarty, Arthur Stewart; goods foreman: Bob Shaw; signalmen:  Paddy Egan, Christy Harney, shunters: Larry Caddan, Paddy Keville; goods yard night porters: Paddy Ward and Mick Duck; porters at passenger station: Michael Coen, Paddy Cox, Denny Davey, Benny Molloy, Paddy O'Connor.

Clerical Staff were: Bill Dooley, Paddy Hickey, Larry Deignan, Jim Carroll, Jack McGivney, John O'Connell, Martin Melly, Winston Algeo and Dave Fleming.

I got to know the clerical staff at Sligo quay on a rota basis. They would come on duty at 6.00am to book the SL&NCR cattle shipments and frozen meat containers for Belfast.

SLIGO, LEITRIM & NORTHERN COUNTIES RAILWAY.

Rail Car Depot _____

RAIL CAR "B"                                    DATE_____

Signed on_____                             Signed off_____

The above Car was handed over to Driver_____

at_____Station on_____195 at_____(time).

1.  Is Engine running satisfactorily ? _____
2.  Is it working on all Cylinders ?   _____
3.  Is Speedometer registering ?       _____
4.  Is Engine revolution counter registering ? _____
5.  Is Self Starter in good order ?    _____
6.  Are Green Tell-Tale lights in Remote Cab in good order ?____
7.  Is Battery in good order ?         _____
8.  Are all lights (inside and outside) working ? _____
9.  Is Gear Selector in good order ?   _____
10. Is Reverse Box Mechanism in good order ?_____
11. Are Brakes in good order ?         _____
12. Is Amp-meter registering correct rate of charge ?_____
13. Give the following readings during trip -

    Maximum Water Temperature_____  Minimum Air Pressure_____

    Minimum Oil Pressure_____   Minimum Vacuum Guage reading_____

    (Reservoir)(Train Pipe)_____

14. Report anything not already mentioned :-




Diesel Oil taken at Enniskillen                          _____galls.
Engine Oil (Densol G.S?Summer) taken at Enniskillen.    _____Quarts
Engine Oil (Densol G. Winter)      "    "    "          _____Quarts
Compressor Oil (Densol G.S.)       "    "    "          _____Quarts
Reverse Box Oil (Red Wormal)       "    "    "          _____Quarts
Axle Box Oil (Red Wormal)          "    "    "          _____Quarts
Exhauster Oil (Castrol X.L.)       "    "    "          _____quarts
Air Filters Oil Densol G.S.)       "    "    "          _____quarts
Self Change Gearbox Oil (Shell C.Y.1) "    "            _____Quarts
Hydraulic Couplings Oil (Shell A.B.11)"    "           _____Quarts
Outside Coupling Rods (Loco Engine)   "    "           _____Quarts
Grease (Castroleose Heavy)            "    "           _____lbs.

                    Driver's Signature_____

This report is to be sent to the Loco. Engineer on completion
of day's working, together with Coaching Bill.

Railcar B, June, 1954, approaching Enniskillen. Photo: N. Sprinks

# CHAPTER NINE

# Railcar B

*Railcar B* was very much part of my life during my years as a guard. A magnificent modern diesel, 107 horsepower car, it was built by Walker Bros., Wigan, England and cost £10,552. SL&NCR acquired it on 9 July 1947. The other two railcars were proving inadequate for the volume of passengers.

Paddy Nevin, an Enniskillen-based locomotive driver, was assigned to drive Railcar B. I remember well the day of its maiden run from Enniskillen to Sligo. I was working at Dromahaire at the time and a great crowd gathered to see it arrive. Approaching the station slowly, the driver and engineer had to check for 'clearance' between it and the passenger platform because it was much wider than the other railcars then in use. Its makers' name was displayed in bold lettering on some of the windows. Among those on board were S.C. Little, General Manager, G.F. Egan, Company Engineer, representatives of the firm who built it and invited guests. Later these guests were entertained to lunch and drinks in the Great Southern hotel, Sligo.

*Railcar B* was an eight wheeled vehicle 47 ft 7$^1$/$_2$ ins. long and it could be driven from either end, which meant that it didn't have to go onto the turntables at Enniskillen and Sligo. Its main body was painted in two-tone green and the roof in white. The cooling system or radiator was positioned in an unusual place – on top of the roof above the main driving cab. This presented a problem when light branches overhanging the line at certain points came into contact with the radiator, causing slight damage. The beech-tree plantation at Dromahaire and the Castlecoole woods between the Weir Bridge and Enniskillen were two places where the contact could happen. The problem was solved temporarily by securing a wooden box around the radiator. However this was not satisfactory because of a reduction in the amount of air needed to cool the radiator and eventually the wooden casing was replaced with a wire mesh.

The railcar had seating accommodation for fifty-nine passengers. Three-seater rows were positioned on each side of the centre gangway. The seats were upholstered in light blue leather. A heavy linoleum, also light blue in colour covered the floor. The windows were fitted with louvre ventilators and the heating system, which was the least satisfactory feature of the railcar, was a continuous copper piping, which ran along the outer side panels. The luggage compartment was situated beside the main driving cab and was used for post office mails, bicycles, parcels and newspapers. The passenger and luggage compartment each had a pair of manually operated sliding doors on the sides of the car. Underneath the passenger doors were two inbuilt folding footsteps, secured by a locking bar when not in use. The only time I used these steps was at Lisgorman halt, where there was no passenger platform.

Paddy Nevin's relief driver was Paddy McTiernan (his brother Tommy was also a driver, based in Manorhamilton). They were the only two drivers who had charge of *Railcar B*. Paddy Nevin was an extremely dedicated worker. He used to come on duty at Enniskillen at 5.30am, have the rail car checked over and then placed down at the departure platform at 6.00am ready for departure at 6.20am. The scheduled time for arrival in Sligo was 8.35am. I myself used to work as Guard on the 6.20am Sligo railcar for Enniskillen as far as Manorhamilton, which was the 'crossing point' for the railcars. There I changed to *Railcar B* and went back to Sligo. Large numbers of school children travelled with us. On arrival in Sligo, Paddy shunted his railcar onto a siding close to the C.I.E. locomotive shed. Then Paddy and I would start immediately to give it a nice 'touch up' for the return journey. Paddy cleaned the windows with a newspaper left behind by one of the passengers, while I borrowed a mop and bucket and liquid soap from the C.I.E. staff. Then having filled the bucket with boiling water from one of the locomotive engines I set to work, washing the floor, and within fifteen minutes the interior looked like 'silver dollars'. Then Paddy shunted the railcar from the siding onto the main running road and down to the departure passenger platform. With all our passengers on board we set out on the journey for Enniskillen at 9.30am, arriving there at 11.45am and leaving again for Sligo at 12.00 noon.

During the summer, many of the passengers travelling on the midday railcar were Scottish holidaymakers. They came overnight by boat and then setting out from Belfast they reached Enniskillen at 11.45am. Usually the railcar was packed and, despite the lack of sleep on the part of many passengers, we were often treated to a sing-song and good conversation. I liked the Scottish passengers; they were very jolly, though at times I didn't know in hell what they were saying! On arrival at Belcoo and Glenfarne they couldn't understand why they were subjected to customs examination. In Glenfarne they had to leave their seats and take their luggage onto the big green customs examination table positioned on the station platform and wait until the customs officers had checked and rummaged through their belongings.

As we sped along, our passengers loved the fact that they had a clear view of the railway track in front of them. This was because the 'rear end' of the railcar was to the forefront with the driver's half-cab built into the passenger section. Sometimes Paddy Nevin liked to 'show off' by leaving his cab. He would do this after the railcar left Ballintogher station and entered into a two mile straight stretch of track towards Collooney. First he set his controls at normal speed with the 'dead man's handle', which could be pinned back into a selected position. (Nowadays on modern trains the 'dead man's handle' is designed to be more fool-proof and if a driver lets go this 'handle' for any reason, the train automatically comes to a halt.) Anyway, having left the cab, Paddy would walk down the long centre aisle, through the luggage compartment and into the main driving cab and then as if with nothing in particular in mind he would stroll back to the forward driving cab and resume his seat. Paddy's saunter might provoke an exchange like this –

"Jock did ye see that – the driver has left us and we're doin' forty-five."

"Ah we'll be alright, take another sup of that good highland whiskey. You're only seein' things."

The Scottish tourists usually returned from Sligo on the 4.00pm railcar because they got an immediate connection for Belfast in Enniskillen.

They dreaded going through customs examination again for many had gifts and souvenirs for their loved ones at home. On arrival at Belcoo they had to present their luggage for H.M. Customs examination. On one occasion a middleaged woman wasn't keen to open her handbag when requested to do so. She finally relented and was very unhappy when forced to pay duty on items of jewellery she had purchased. I can still see her snapping her handbag shut and then taking a swipe with it at the official, narrowly missing his head. She danced with rage on the platform before boarding the train. It was hell to listen to her on the rest of the journey to Enniskillen.

I remember some of the Scottish women telling me that they were happy enough going home 'stony broke'. In their workplace they had a savings club into which they put a pound or two each week. These savings were then used for big occasions during the year, particularly the annual holidays and the New Year festivities.

*Railcar B* was known affectionately by railway staff and school children as 'Paddy Nevin's railcar'. Indeed, Paddy was reluctant to take his annual holidays in case everything didn't go well in his absence! *Railcar B* was stabled in its shed at Enniskillen awaiting disposal after the railway closed in 1957. Then the following year it was purchased by CIE and painted in its new company's colours – black and tan with a white strip, and given fleet number 2509. For many years afterwards it operated on branch-line passenger services, including rail tours. It was also used for training CIE drivers. After it was taken out of service it lay for a time on one of the sidings in Limerick Junction. Today it can be found on a siding in Mallow, Co. Cork with its windows broken and its body rusting away – a  sad ending to a wonderful piece of rolling stock.

I have gone on two occasions, August 1988 and June 1991 to Mallow station to see it. As I looked at it, many memories of its bygone glory days ran through my mind. When I turned my back to walk away I could feel a sense of sadness creep over me. It was like leaving a graveyard. From the passenger platform I looked at it again for the last time hoping that maybe sometime it might be miraculously restored to its former glory, once more wearing its coat of two-toned green.

Railcar B, May 1953, approaching Manorhamilton from Sligo.
Photo: N. Sprinks

'Sir Henry' approaching Manorhamilton, 27 May 1953.
Crewed by Tommy McTiernan & Paddy Hugh Keaney. Photo: N. Sprinks

# CHAPTER TEN

# The Railway Men

## *Tommy McTiernan*

Tommy McTiernan was one of the great characters among the rail-waymen. He was very stout and went by the nickname 'Curley Wee'. There was a saying among workers which went as follows,
"Who is working the market train to Sligo today?"
"Ah, sure it's Curley Wee and Larry Lee."

Based in Manorhamilton he travelled on the morning railcar to Dromahaire to take over the 6.30am cattle train from his Sligo counterpart and drive it to Enniskillen. The school going children who got on the railcar at Lisgorman halt got to know him very well and constantly teased him about one particular engine which Tommy hated to work on. This was a GNR engine No. 28A, hired by SL&NCR and known in its earlier days as the *'Wexford'*. It was said that Tommy, who was quite moody at times, would take the day off rather than work on it. Indeed it was quite unsuitable for the Sligo-Enniskillen line because of its long coal tender. It was very difficult to get its steam pressure to work properly despite great efforts on the part of the fireman. Time was frequently lost en route, which had serious consequences for the shipments of cattle to be despatched out of Enniskillen.

For some reason best known to himself Tommy always called the the engine *'The Old Dungannon'*. Sometimes one of the school children would ask "How is the Old Dungannon steaming this weather. Do you think its her that's hauling your train today Tommy?"
"I just don't know but I'll know soon enough", Tommy used to reply.
Owen Rooney would join in the conversation about the hated engine with the remark that Tommy had her "on the wrong diet". I remember one morning that Tommy was too late into Enniskillen for

Left to Right: Peter Gillmurray(Foreman Mechanic),
Tommie Marren(Driver), Dominic Connolly(Office) and
Paddy Hugh Keaney(Driver). Photo: D.Murray

the GNR 'shipper' cattle train for Belfast. S.C. Little, our General Manager called him aside:

"Driver, what went wrong this morning?"

"I did my best sir".

"Your best wasn't good enough on this occasion driver."

Sometimes Tommy and his fireman Bernie Gilgunn left Manorhamilton at 5.30am with 'light' engine i.e. with no rolling stock of any kind attached, to pick up a special cattle train in Collooney. At such an early hour some gatekeepers would not be up. One morning Tommy and Bernie arrived at a particular level crossing to find the gates closed. As Bernie alighted to open them, Tommy noticed the gatekeeper's fine garden of vegetables and decided to help himself to a few varieties which glistened in the morning dew. Then full steam ahead he gave two loud train whistles to remind the gatekeeper that it was time to rise.

One morning, in Collooney, my cattle train was ready to leave. Station Master Paddy Denning, informed us that he would request the Manorhamilton engine, driven by Tommy McTiernan to bank us. Banking meant that another engine assisted your train to get over steep inclines by pushing from behind– a  procedure which saved valuable time. The exchange of whistles was acknowledged by both drivers and Tommy prepared to bank us for about three miles over the Ballygawley and Castledargan steep incline. All was going well until he seemed to lose contact with our train about one and a half miles from Collooney station. Tommy decided to make contact again and Michael Harte from Sligo, who was a fireman based in Enniskillen, and myself were terrified in the Guard's van as we saw this engine coming towards us at speed, its black smoke churning up from its chimney and the steam gushing from its sides. We braced ourselves for the impending impact. Just as our train was crossing the bridge spanning the Sligo/Drumshanbo road beside Ballygawley village, Tommy's engine hit us with a violent bang. It was a miracle that our train wasn't derailed. If derailment had occurred the rear end of the cattle train would have toppled down onto the main road beneath. The fact that a passenger coach with its well-sprung buffers was placed in front of my Guards van did soften the impact. However I was shaken and sore for many days afterwards.

Tommy was well-known for his wit. On one occasion he was travelling back as a passenger on the evening railcar from Enniskillen. He got into conversation with an old Yank wearing a large cowboy hat who entertained everybody on board to a great picture of what life was like in America. He described the magnificence of the buildings and how quickly they could be constructed – literally in a couple of days according to himself. He particularly stressed the enormous American restaurants. After leaving Enniskillen he glimpsed the Cole monument.

"Hey man", he said, to Tommy, "what's that there?"

"That's the Cole monument and wouldn't it make an ideal pepper canister for one of your restaurants over there?" Tommy replied. There was silence for a good part of the journey after that, that is until

Left to Right: Paddy Hugh Keaney, Joe Neilan and Author
Michael Hamilton at Enniskillen. Photo: M.Keaney

the train was passing the White Fathers' College at Blacklion. The
Yank couldn't restrain himself and enquired what it was.

"Well I don't know sir what it is. It wasn't there this morning when
I was passing with my train," Tommy exclaimed!

I remember how he used to persuade young lads who joined the railway in Manorhamilton to bring in eggs to him.

"Tell your mother to send in two dozen hen eggs for the men here.
This is an old custom we have here and it will bring you  good luck in
your new job," was the request to the raw  recruit.

Tommy McTiernan was indeed a rare character.


## Martin  Brannigan

Martin Brannigan was a very popular train guard on the SL&NCR.
Standing about six feet three inches he was known to us as 'Boss
Brannigan'. He went into railway folklore for a number of incidents, one
of which was his involvement in a twelfth of July Orange celebration.

Martin arrived in Enniskillen on the morning of the twelfth on an early
morning cattle special from Collooney. It was a rule that crew on early
morning trains were entitled to cheese sandwiches and a bottle of

Guinness in the saloon on the GNR platform. Martin duly collected his docket from the General Manager's office and as he was going into the bar a GNR special train arrived from Ballinamallard, carrying a few hundred people on their way to the rally in the Broad Meadow. Some of the passengers went into the bar and invited Martin to a few drinks with them. After a while one of them said to him, "You'd be an ideal man to beat the big Lambeg drum on our way to the field. You're the right height as well".

Martin, who had a number of drinks by now, saw no reason why not, so he was harnessed up to the big drum and marched off with the Orangemen, through Enniskillen, to the Broad Meadow, where the Sports Forum Centre is now located. Sometime later, exhausted by his exertions, he decided that it was time to be getting back to the station. However it was decided that he be relieved of his duty run on the 1.40pm. railcar to Sligo. Sam Fiddes, clerical officer in the General Manager's office was detailed to go as far as Manorhamilton, as relief guard, and foreman John Ward took over from there. Except for a sore head Martin was none the worse for his experience.

Glenfarne Station Master Paddy Denning
with Railcar 2A. Photo: H. Johnston

Left to Right: John Howe, Jimmy McHugh, Bertie Hegarty and Tommie
Marren at Enniskillen Station, 24 May 1955. Photo: N. Sprinks.

On another occasion the 'Boss' was shunting busy cattle wagons and
getting his train ready. It was one of those days where a number of
cattle specials had departed earlier. Martin's train would be the last to
leave. However in the course of shunting on the siding known as
Markree cattle loading bank, the engine, 28A, hired from GNR,
became derailed twice. This engine, because of its very long coal tender, was unsuitable for the SL&NCR line. The traffic manager in the
General Manager's office became concerned about the late departure
of the train, since it was carrying an important shipment of cattle. The
station master in Collooney was advised by Martin to telegraph the
traffic manager with the following message:
 *On again, off again, gone again.*
 *Brannigan.*

Left to Right: Johnny Gaffney, Bernie Hegarty,
Dominic Connolly and Gerry O'Connor. Photo: M. Keaney

Left to Right: Jimmy McHugh, Glenfarne,
two GNR Staff and Paddy Hugh Keaney. Photo: M.Keaney

Martin always managed to acquire a free raincoat every year. This resulted from a regulation of British Customs who issued their officers with new raincoats at the beginning of the summer. When passing through Belcoo, Martin would shout to Gerry Rasdale, a very tall customs officer – "Health to wear officer– any chance of the old one?" The old coat would be waiting for the 'Boss' on the return journey from Enniskillen.

On one occasion when I was working in Dromahaire, Martin arrived with his goods train of twelve CIE wagons, each carrying twelve tons of Indian corn for Hosie's mill. To save time he decided to unhook the wagons and let them roll into the mill on their own. As they picked up too much speed, I ran down from the signal-box to try to 'pin down' some wagon handbrakes, but to no avail. There was no way of preventing them hitting the buffer stops. Behind these stops, Mrs Lambe the station master's wife used to scatter dry ashes in which her flock of Rhode Island reds loved to burrow and scrape. When the speeding wagons violently struck the buffer stops a shower of ashes and the screeching hens were despatched into the Breffni air! However, Martin was quite philosophical about the incident, remarking that "there's nothing bad but could be worse."

## SLIGO, LEITRIM & NORTHERN COUNTIES RAILWAY.
### WORKING TIME TABLE.

The following service of SCHEDULED TRAINS and RAIL CARS will operate from MONDAY, 5th September, 1955 until further notice.

### UP TRAINS:

|  |  | Rail Car a.m. | Live Stock & Goods a.m. | Goods a.m. | Rail Car p.m. |
|---|---|---|---|---|---|
| Sligo | dep. | 6.20 | 6.30 | 11.15 | 4. 0 |
| Ballysodare | arr. | 6.30 | 6.45 | 11.36 | 4.10 |
| -do- | dep. | 6.31 | 6.47 | 11.46 | 4.13 |
| Collooney | arr. | 6.36 | 6.52 | 11.51 | 4.17 |
| -do- | dep. | 6.38T | 7.20S | 12.10S | 4.20S |
| Dromahair | arr. | 6.56 | 7.40 | 12.30 | 4.38 |
| -do- | dep. | 7. 0S | 7.45T | 12.40S | 4.40S |
| Manorhamilton | arr. | 7.20 | 8. 5 | 1. 0 | 4.58 |
| -do- | dep. | 7.25T | 8.15T | 1.30S | 5. 0S |
| Glenfarne | arr. | 7.43 | 8.35 | 1.50 | 5.18 |
| -do- | dep. | 7.45T | 8.55T | 1.55S | 5.20S |
| Belcoo | arr. | 7.58 | 9.10 | 2.10 | 5.35 |
| -do- | dep. | 8. 5T | 9.30S | 3.10T | 5.45S |
| Florencecourt | arr. | 8.19 | 9.45 | 3.25 | 5.59 |
| -do- | dep. | 8.20T | 9.46S | 3.30T | 6. 0S |
| Enniskillen | arr. | 8.35 | 10. 0 | 3.45 | 6.15 |

### DOWN TRAINS:

|  |  | Rail Car a.m. | Rail Car p.m. | Goods p.m. | Mixed p.m. |
|---|---|---|---|---|---|
| Enniskillen | dep. | 6.20S | 1.45T | 2. 0S | 7.20T |
| Florencecourt | arr. | 6.32 | 1.57 | 2.15 | 7.32 |
| -do- | dep. | 6.33S | 1.58T | 2.18S | 7.33T |
| Belcoo | arr. | 6.48 | 2.13 | 2.33 | 7.48 |
| -do- | dep. | 6.50S | 2.18T | 2.48S | 7.53T |
| Glenfarne | arr. | 7. 2 | 2.30 | 3. 3 | 8. 5 |
| -do- | dep. | 7. 5S | 2.35T | 3.15S | 8.10T |
| Manorhamilton | arr. | 7.23 | 2.55 | 3.35 | 8.28 |
| -do- | dep. | 7.26S | 2.57S | 5. 5T | 8.30S |
| Dromahair | arr. | 7.44 | 3.15 | 5.25 | 8.48 |
| -do- | dep. | 7.50S | 3.17S | 5.35T | 8.50S |
| Collooney | arr. | 8.10 | 3.37 | 5.55 | 9.10 |
| -do- | dep. | 8.15 | 3.37 | 6.15 | 9.15 |
| Ballysodare | arr. | 8.20 | 3.42 | 6.25 | 9.20 |
| -do- | dep. | 8.25 | 3.45 | 6.45 | 9.25 |
| Sligo | arr. | 8.35 | 3.55 | 7. 0 | 9.35 |

S. stands for Train Staff ) - in above Table.
T.   "    "    "    Ticket )

The 6.20 a.m. down Rail Car to cross 6.20.a.m..Up Rail Car at MANORHAMILTON and 6.30 a.m. Up train at DROMAHAIR.

The 1.45 p.m. down Rail Car to cross 11.15 a.m. Up Goods train at BELCOO.

The 2. 0 p.m. down Goods train to cross the 11.15 a.m. Up Goods train at BELCOO and 4.0 p.m. Up Rail Car at MANORHAMILTON.

Rail Cars will STOP at all Halts, if required. The 7.20 p.m. down train will stop at ABOHILL, KILLWAKERRILL and BALLINTOGHER, if required, by notice to Guard at preceding stations, but this service will cease to call at Lisgorman and Ballygawley. The times shewn as per Public Notice for the 7.20 p.m. down service are indicated when this service is worked by Rail Car, but it is understandable that further time may be required when worked by steam as a Mixed train.

CERTAIN OTHER INSTRUCTIONS SET FORTH IN SERVICE TIME TABLE DATED JUNE, 1936 TO BE STILL OBSERVED.

S. C. LITTLE,
General Manager.

August, 1955.

'Hazelwood' at Manorhamilton with driver Tommie Marren. Photo: N. Sprinks

# CHAPTER ELEVEN

## Mobile Self Catering

CIE and GNR engine crews and train guards coming on duty at Sligo and Enniskillen brought their meals in large wicker baskets. Also attached to their baskets were their tea-drinking accessories – white enamel billy cans. Each can had a deep lid and handle and was used as a drinking cup. Since the crews frequently stayed overnight at various depots to match their rostered duties, the baskets were usually well full. Train crews who had to stay away from their depots experienced grim enough conditions in the dormitories attached to these depots. Often a good night's sleep was impossible. SL&NCR train crews were lucky in that they didn't have to stay overnight, and compared to our CIE and GNR colleagues our food rations were much less.

When we took a break for a meal the self-catering process was put into operation. First, the well-blackened tea can was filled with water, then hung on the long-handled crooked end of the fire picker (which was used for stoking the coal-fire) and thrust into the engine's raging firebox. When the water was boiled, tea from the lovely tea/sugar canisters, which had a lid at each end, was put into the tea can. If a fry was on the menu a few hygiene regulations had to be observed. The fireman's coal shovel was washed clean with scalding water from the engine's boiler. When it was as clean as a hound's tooth, the rashers, eggs, sausages and black pudding were placed on it. Then, holding the shovel steady the cook gently thrust it into the hungry firebox with its flames ready to jump out at you. When the contents were done on one side, they were turned and in a matter of minutes the meal was ready for serving.

On a cold winter's morning I often got the fireman to fry some salami for me. Salami was new at the time and my dear old landlady seemed to have it on the lunch menu more often than I care to remember. Train crews never took proper rest after their meals. They usually gulped them down and went back to work. Indeed they worked so hard that they were frequently hungry. This was especially true in harsh weather conditions. They often ate snacks as they speeded along. I never met a railway man who hadn't a good appetite and many of them were fond of good porter which helped to wash down the coal dust!

One man, who certainly had a sizeable appetite was Owen Rooney, who was attached to Manorhamilton station. When he worked as a milesman he travelled on the early morning Enniskillen railcar, from Manorhamilton and dismounted at the Lisgorman halt. From there he inspected the line all the way back to Manorhamilton. He carried a large army surplus haversack on his back, and you couldn't but notice that it was always bulging.

On the journey to Lisgorman the schoolchildren might ask, "What's the packing like today, Owen?" To which he would reply, "I have a large soda cake, smothered in country butter and a 'junt' of boiled bacon." When he met up with other milesmen working the same section they usually retired to a local farmhouse, where the woman of the house made tea for them and invited them to sit at the kitchen table. Owen duly opened his haversack, "made an attack", on the provisions and washed the lot down with three mugs of tea.

"Lord, Owen you have a fair stroke", one of the men might say.

"Ah, sure men, you know an empty sack won't stand up," was Owen's stock reply.

After work he often retired to the pub with someone he happened to meet and treated himself to a few pints of Guinness. Then he'd go home to tackle the dinner, which consisted, in his own words, of a 'borgue of kangers' – meaning about twelve or fourteen potatoes and a 'bellace' of buttermilk, that is about three mug-fulls. He duly despatched whatever else might be on the menu as well.

Railway men might have great appetites but, they were also very alert. In fact they had to be. When I started to work first, I often wondered how engine crews could know their bearings in the darkness or in snowy or foggy conditions. The two oil-lit headlamps were really of little use in establishing your location. The drivers especially, after years of experience, became familiar with every mile of the track and were aware of the exact place they were passing through at any given time. Therefore they were on the look-out for the signals protecting the level crossing gates and for any emergency that might occur. As a train guard I developed the art of knowing my location. A keen ear often gave you the clue at night. I had to be alert as one of my duties was to fling out train notices at each of the level crossing gate houses.

Incidentally, the uniforms for railway staff of the SL&NCR in the Republic, were made by John Ireland of Dublin. Staff in the north were supplied by McTaggart of Glasgow. However, the top coats, or great coats as they were called, for all SL&NCR guards were also made by McTaggart. This caused a slight problem for me and the other guards based in the Republic. We collected the coats in the manager's office in Enniskillen but couldn't bring them across the border in their wrapping paper – otherwise the customs officials would insist on your paying duty on them. I remember the first time I got my coat, Harry Taylor, our traffic manager, said to me:

"For heaven's sake, take that coat out of its parcel and wear it until you get past Glenfarne station, even if the sun is cracking the stones."

The guard's coat was very finely made, and it was lined with heavy, blue/grey herringbone cloth. I received a new coat every four years!

## DELAYS TO TRAINS.

Station Masters must send to the General Manager's Office Special Reports of Delays to Trains, exceeding five minutes, at their Stations beyond the time allowed. Every effort must be made to ensure punctuality in the running of the Trains. Tickets must not be issued after the Trains have arrived at the Stations, and Station Masters must be upon the platform on the arrival of Trains to see that the business is done with despatch.

## SPEED OF TRAINS.

The speed of Passenger Trains is not to exceed *thirty* miles per hour, and Goods and Cattle Trains *twenty* miles per hour.

The speed on approaching a Station should not exceed *ten* miles per hour, and be reduced to *eight* miles per hour on passing over the Facing Points.

Engine Drivers must be prepared to pull up, if at any Station the Distant or Home Signals are against them; but special caution is to be observed when approaching Sligo, Ballysodare and Enniskillen Stations.

The speed of Trains round the curves between Enniskillen and No. 3 Gate and Boheveney, as also Kilmakerrill Summit, and those in Lisgorman, Dark Valley, Socks and Drumlease, is not to exceed *ten* miles per hour.

No Train or Engine to cross the Erne Bridge near Enniskillen at a speed exceeding *five* miles per hour, and in all cases with steam shut off.

\* \* The Guards are to be most careful to have with them, when on duty, the prescribed Number of DETONATING SIGNALS, and they are *immediately to go back to protect their Trains* if brought to a stand, even when within a Distant Signal. The distances at which Detonators are to be laid are—one Detonator a quarter of a mile from his Train, one half a mile from his Train, and three, ten yards apart, not less than three-quarters of a mile from his Train, respectively.—*See Rule 217 of General Rule Book.* ANY NEGLECT OF THIS PRECAUTION WILL RENDER THE GUARD LIABLE TO IMMEDIATE DISMISSAL AND IMPRISONMENT.

# CHAPTER TWELVE

# The Near Accidents

One of the scariest events of my time on the railway involved two cattle trains on one of which I was guard. It was the harvest time of the year - the busiest season – for the cattle trade and my train, after been loaded with about three hundred animals in Collooney was on its way to Enniskillen. I remember that the morning was showery with strong gusts of wind as we pulled into Manorhamilton station. We spent the usual time in the station, fifteen minutes, checking the wagons to see that the cattle were "on their feet". The crew also took on board the required amount of water for the engine at the water column provided for all 'up' trains to Enniskillen.

I was well aware that a cattle train had gone ahead of us having entered the Manorhamilton/Glenfarne section of line an hour and a quarter earlier. This train should have 'cleared' this section in thirty five minutes or so. Our driver Tommy McTiernan having received his train-ticket as authority to enter the Glenfarne section, from the foreman there, reversed his train out of the station to a place known as the "big black sheds" on the Dromahaire side. This procedure was necessary in the case of heavy trains to get up speed to tackle the steep hill known as Williamson's Bank one and a half miles away in the town land of Lisnagroagh. This hill was dreaded by all engine drivers especially those in charge of heavy trains. Tommy, on full steam ahead, started his run down through the station and out into the Glenfarne section. Then he and his ever watchful fireman Bernie Gilgunn spotted the rear of the cattle train which had gone before us, slowly moving back towards us. As Tommy and Bernie gradually brought our train to a halt, the clanging of the buffers, as the wagons made contact, could be heard clearly over a mile away. A terrible accident had been avoided. If we had left the station five minutes earlier there would have been a certain collision and with about six hundred head of cattle involved the result could have been catastrophic. The first train had failed on first and second attempts to get over Williamson's Bank and the crew then decided to reverse with caution back to Manorhamilton station.

There were now two cattle trains in Manorhamilton, and the station master telegraphed his counterpart in Dromahaire to hold the third train in his station, pending further instructions, since both 'up' and 'down' lines were occupied in Manorhamilton. There was a lot of agitation in the station that morning – some railwaymen were white faced, but gradually calm returned and we breathed a sigh of relief, knowing things could have been a lot worse.

Weather conditions played a big part in the failure of the first cattle train. The line was wet and the gusting wind caused the free flowing dry sand from the engine's sand boxes to scatter to one side and not make contact with the rails. The driver now had to contend with slipping or 'wheel spin' resulting in a crucial loss of power. The ensuing enquiry had two important issues to investigate: the final clearance of the first cattle train in the Manorhamilton/Glenfarne section and the acceptance of a second train into the section when there was a train already on it. The results of the enquiry remained a secret throughout the remaining years of the railway. In later years when I used to meet the fireman, Bernie Gilgunn (R.I.P.) who was largely instrumental in preventing the accident, we talked at length of our near miss and what could have been a dark day in the history of SL&NCR.

During my time as a guard on the railway, I experienced three derailments, on different occasions, involving the same railcar – *Railcar 2A*. Each of the three took place outside Manorhamilton on the Dromahaire section. One of the incidents took place at Larkfield, about two miles outside Manorhamilton station. As the driver, Jack Connolly, approached a left hand curve the two front wheels suddenly became derailed. All on board experienced a bump but there were no injuries. I sent word back to the station master in Manorhamilton informing him of what had occurred and a bus with staff was sent out immediately to the nearest pick up point for the railcar passengers, their luggage and also for the post office mails. The bus called in at all the stations en route to Sligo and none of us was any the worse for the experience. The derailed railcar was speedily put back on the line by a breakdown crew operating from Manorhamilton and taken back to the station to be checked over for damage. An inspection of the place of derailment revealed that the line had spread, meaning that it was out of gauge. This had been caused by a goods train which had passed over the section two hours earlier. This goods train was hauled by one of the two new engines the company had acquired – the *Lough Erne* or the *Lough Melvin*. Permanent way staff were aware that these engines were somewhat tight when entering sharp curves, pushing the line slightly out of gauge. It was necessary to regularly inspect such curves for damage.

The second derailment occurred when I was working on the 9.30am Sligo to Enniskillen service. On entering Manorhamilton a wooden boarding which was placed upright alongside the 'Bond Stores' close to the rail tracks, was blown onto the line by a freak gust of wind in front of the railcar, causing its derailment. Luckily neither the driver Jimmy Keaney nor any of those on board were injured. The passengers were taken down to the station waiting rooms until the railcar was put back into service. It is remarkable that this run would normally be done by *Railcar B* which was out of service on this occasion.

The last time in which I had experience of a derailment occurred in the month of October. I was guard on the 1.45pm Enniskillen to Sligo service. At this time of the year the grass supply in the nearby fields was getting very scarce and there was always a danger that cattle would 'thieve' onto the railway embankments, where there was usually plenty of grass. We were only about a mile outside Manorhamilton station and rounding a curve in the line when two big Hereford bullocks, who had been grazing on the embankment dashed onto the tracks, having been startled by the noise of the railcar. Our driver, Joe Dunbar, hadn't sufficient time to bring his railcar to a halt; a collision occurred and the two front wheels of the car came to rest two feet above the rail on the bodies of the bullocks, whose dying cries were pitiful to hear. The passengers remained very calm before they were taken off safely. Three of those who travelled with us that day were Mrs Mary Keaney, wife of Jimmy Keaney a train driver with the company; her son Liam and her daughter Maura. They were travelling from Kilmakerrill to Sligo.

All emergencies were put into operation to deal with the situation and the remainder of this service was undertaken by bus. A full investigation took place; the fencing was carefully checked, to establish where the cattle had entered onto the line. Claims for the loss of the animals were made against the railway company by their owner and counterclaims for damages and expenses were entered by the company. I had to write several reports to the company regarding the accident and the case went on for months. I was glad to hear when the book was closed on this unfortunate occurrence.

# CHAPTER THIRTEEN

# Smuggling

Smuggling the white batch loaf from Northern Ireland into the south was big business during the war years and for some time afterwards. The flour up north produced a much whiter and better quality loaf than the yellowish loaf in the Republic. Almost every day there would be requests from people to bring back white bread from Enniskillen. In order to do this it was necessary to have ready-made places to hide the goods and the space underneath the rear seating of *Railcar 2A* provided the answer. This seating could be raised and beneath was a false bottom. In here was stored a container of the dry sand which was used to prevent the wheels of the railcar skidding on wet rails on the application of brakes. The bread was packed in here alongside the container and the false lid was fitted. The hiding place was never detected by any of the customs officers on either side of the border.

Tommy McTiernan also engaged in a little smuggling. He usually brought back about six white plain loaves, concealing them under a big black overcoat until he had cleared customs. Indeed most of the customs officers, both British and Irish were well aware of what he had under his coat. Sometimes at Glenfarne, customs officer Tony Gaughan would remark, "God Tommy you seem to be putting on a lot of beef this weather. It's time you started to slim a bit". After leaving Glenfarne Tommy took the bread from under his coat and transferred it to the overhead baggage racks.

*Coach No.9*, a beautiful carriage, was frequently used for smuggling. It was fitted with bogie type wheels for smooth travel. Power lighting was provided by the coach itself. A dynamo was affixed beneath the frame of the coach and a pulley-belt led from the dynamo to a pulley-wheel, which was attached to the axle of one of the bogie wheels. Thus, electricity was generated when the train was in motion. Two large

Railcar 2A at Belcoo Station. Second from left, H.M. Customs Officer William Fletcher checking Passengers luggage.

wooden boxes, which held wet batteries charged by the pulley arrangement, were fitted beneath the frame of the coach. One of these boxes had more space than was required by the batteries and was often filled with smuggled goods. In its day this box carried whiskey, cigarettes and chickens, mostly north-bound. On many occasions I was asked by nervous passengers to hide things for them. Nurses heading back to the Royal Victoria Hospital in Belfast were regular smugglers. I dreaded coming up to Christmas as I would be snowed under by requests from people anxious to post Christmas parcels in Northern Ireland. These parcels usually contained chickens, lamb, pork or butter.

Apart from its smuggling facilities *Coach 9* was quite luxurious. The first class sections were beautifully carpeted and sliding doors separated smoking and non-smoking accommodation. The seating was pale green with pink floral design. Each first class compartment took eight passengers in comfort. On the walls hung pictures of local interest: the Abbey Hotel, Dromahaire; Florencecourt House and views of the lakes such as Lough Gill, Lough Erne, Glencar and Melvin. Heavy, thick glass mirrors were placed over each seating arrangement. The roof lights were three-pronged with ornamented glass shades; matching wall lights were placed over each seat. There were ten lights in all for the comfort of passengers.

Sometimes smuggling activities could go badly wrong and prove very costly. One of the most expensive examples which I know of occurred on a train travelling from Enniskillen to Sligo. The driver and fireman were topping up the coal tender with about one and a half tons of coal at the loading bank, when they were approached by a man with a request to smuggle a big parcel. This parcel contained several yards of men's suit material. At this time, material of this type was very scarce and very expensive and apparently it was more readily available in the the north of Ireland and less costly. The fireman and the driver agreed to take the parcel and they told the man that they would bury it beneath the coal. He was delighted.

"There's the price of a few pints for ye for this transaction", he said.

The driver and the fireman placed the parcel beneath the coal and brought the engine down to the passenger platform to pick up its passenger coach. They also had to pick up the remainder of the train which consisted of fifteen empty cattle wagons and guard's van. In order to do this the driver, as usual, left the platform with his engine and passenger coach, then proceeded over Tempo Road bridge and reversed back to hook up to the other portion of the train which was placed on a siding. Just as the train was about to leave, the shunter ran up to the driver and told him that he and his fireman had been seen hiding a huge parcel in the coal bunker .

"If I were ye, ye better watch out for yerselves", he said.

On the journey to Belcoo the two men decided to take the parcel to the surface of the coal and if the worst came to the worst they would be in a position to dispose of it quickly. On arrival in Belcoo they spotted a policeman and customs officer walking smartly towards the engine. Without any hesitation the fireman opened the firebox door and the driver flung the parcel into the bright roaring fire, the light of which was so intense that the naked eye could not look at it. The customs officer boarded the engine and asked both men if they had any goods to declare. They said they hadn't and he then proceeded to spike the coal with a steel rod but to no avail. Hundreds of pounds worth of material had gone up in smoke.

Another incident, quite less serious, occurred on the 6.30am train ex-Sligo on which I was guard. The smuggler got on board at Manorhamilton. He had three pounds of butter with him for relations in the North. Since he wasn't comfortable with keeping the butter beside him, it was suggested to him that he hide it behind one of the heating cylinders positioned beneath the the seating. This seemed to be a perfect arrangement but unfortunately things did not turn out well for the man. At Glenfarne station some passengers complained that the coach was very cold – it was the end of September. The complaint was passed on to me and I, in accordance with my duties, passed it on to the fireman. He duly hooked up the steam heating from the engine to the coach. In a matter of minutes the heating cylinders were warmed up. When the train arrived at Enniskillen the man leaned down to recover his butter only to find that it was an oily mess dripping onto the floor. I still remember the disappointment and dismay on his face.

Apart from smuggling, it was amazing the variety of messages people would request from employees of the railway. One man regularly requested *The News of the World*, from Enniskillen, since it was banned in the Republic.

"Ah!, there's great tips for the horses in that paper,", he'd say, even though it was well known he never backed a horse in his life!

Another regular request was for 'cut-throat' razors to be taken into Barton-Smiths in Sligo to be 'ground' or sharpened.

"Tell them to have it ready for Saturday, for I could do with a shave for Sunday Mass," I was always reminded.

On many occasions I collected driving licences for people. They would give me the filled-in application form and five shillings and I collected the licence at Sligo Courthouse. I also used to collect licences for some people in Northern Ireland. I still can't figure out that one!

Leaving in watches for repair to jewellers, was a constant request and also posting the English 'Football Coupons' in Northern Ireland. We even had to pay peoples' 'Rates Demand', because they'd tell you they couldn't be bothered doing it themselves! But one request I always turned down, was from schoolchildren, to bring in 'bangers and squibs', at Hallowe'en. It was, of course, illegal to import them into the Republic and there were always disappointed faces.

6.30 am train ex Sligo at Glenfarne Station. Photo: M.Davies

# CHAPTER FOURTEEN

# Passengers

Down through the years a *Special Excursion Train* ran from Enniskillen to Sligo on Garland Sunday. This was to facilitate passengers who wished to visit the Holy Well and participate in the ceremonies there. On arrival in Sligo, they took a bus out to the well from the station. The train started on its return journey from Sligo at 7.30pm. As it sped past our house, many people used to lean out of the carriage windows wildly waving their arms. For many, this was their very first time to travel by train.

Garland Sunday was a big day for me, as a child. The previous evening my father checked the bicycles. The chains were tightened and oiled, the brakes were tested and the tyres examined. Finally, the puncture repair kit was placed in the pouch hanging from the saddle. Preparations, such as these, were very necessary as the road which myself and my father travelled wasn't tarred. The reason we cycled was to attend the first Mass at the well at 6.00am. After the Mass I visited the stalls where dilusk was available in large quantities. I brought back to my grandmother, at her request, a bottle of Holy Well water and a big bag of dilusk, which she boiled in milk. Its taste was beautiful and the rich smell hung around the house for hours.

Each year, in July, hundreds of boy scouts, superintended by their scout master, travelled from Belfast to their large camp site at Lissadell, Co. Sligo. They arrived in Enniskillen by GNR train. Then they rushed across the platform to board the special SL&NCR steam train for Sligo. You could see the excitement on their faces and they seemed to enjoy leaving one train and scrambling into another. They were extremely well behaved however, which made the task of the scout master quite easy.

The wagons, containing their equipment and also food and drink, were shunted off the GNR train and attached to ours. So then it was off on the pleasant journey to Sligo. On arrival at the station, there was more excitement when they saw a fleet of CIE buses and a lorry for their equipment waiting to complete the journey to Lissadell. After a week or so they made the trip to Belfast – apparently quite happy with their holiday in Sligo.

One of the busiest times of the year for the SL&NCR was late September and early October. The number travelling by rail was greatly increased by the returning migratory labourers from Scotland. During the summer, hundreds of them left the west of Ireland and particularly North Mayo for the seasonal potato picking. The railcar services had to be doubled or even trebled to take the large influx of people making their way home. They usually carried great amounts of luggage, including big trunks and wooden boxes. You'd think they had half of Scotland home with them! Confusion usually reigned in Belcoo and Glenfarne where the customs checks took place. Usually the cases were secured with ropes which took a long time to untie. A lot of time was spent explaining to the customs officials what each item of luggage contained. The schedule could not be adhered to when the potato pickers were on board. The train was due to arrive at 3.55pm in order to catch the 4.00pm buses to Crossmolina, Blacksod, Westport, Ballina, Kiltimagh and Bangor Erris. Since there usually wasn't a hope of making the connection, I would take note of all the passengers travelling onwards to other destinations and then phone ahead to Sligo requesting the buses to wait. The buses, in turn, were delayed due to the vast amounts of luggage to be handled and accommodated.

The 1.40pm rail car from Enniskillen to Sligo was often called the 'Honeymoon Railcar'. Many newly married couples boarded it at Glenfarne, Manorhamilton and Dromahaire. Having arrived in Sligo, they might stay overnight or continue on their journey by bus to places such as Westport or Galway. Some availed of the evening mail train to Dublin. It was the porter's job to sweep and clean the railcar in preparation for its next service.

"There's been another execution today," he'd say, when he'd see the confetti strewn on the seats and floor of the vehicle.

I remember one honeymoon couple arriving at Glenfarne Station to board the railcar on which I was guard. They were accompanied by all the wedding guests who rushed forward to hug and kiss them before their departure. The passing of time has taken its sad toll on a number of those happy honeymooners of long ago. In the case of many that I knew personally, only one partner survives.

The trains were crowded with people at Christmas. Families packed the platforms along the line waiting to greet their relatives. Also present, were the curious onlookers, anxious to note the latest arrivals. As the emigrants alighted from the train, their relatives rushed forward to kiss and hug them. Then the luggage – and there always seemed to be an enormous amount of it – was grasped by willing hands and carried to waiting taxis. The joy of pre-Christmas turned to sadness when it was time for the visitors to return. As the train was moving off they would lean out of the carriage windows to exchange the last few tearful words with their loved ones. Then, waving their hankies until the platform disappeared from view, they settled back on their seats and brushed away the remaining tears from their eyes.

On one occasion, I had to work late on Christmas Eve i.e. on the 4.00pm railcar, Sligo to Enniskillen and back on the 7.20pm steam train. In Enniskillen extra coaches had to be attached to the 7.20pm to accommodate the huge numbers of extra passengers. Our departure was delayed as we awaited the GNR connecting trains from Belfast, Derry and Clones. As a result it was 8.00pm when we left the station. There were further delays in Belcoo and Glenfarne due to customs checks. The driver did make up time on the remainder of the journey arriving at Sligo at 10.00pm.

I still remember that night very well. I opened the big inside doors of the guards or brake van at the rear of the train and stepped out under the veranda. I could see the great countryside dotted with hundreds of flickering lights as the Christmas candles lit up the windows of the houses. As we sped along, the lights seemed to change and it was breathtaking to see them high up on the mountainsides. The whole scene was like a starry sky turned upside down. At that time of course there was no electricity and there were many more houses in country areas.

Coming up to Christmas Tommy McTiernan got very generous with the Company coal. When passing some of the gatehouses he would push a few large lumps off the footplate of his engine for collection by the gatekeeper. I remember when it landed on our street it would be swept along by the airstream of the train. Tommy's coal was a novelty in the country at that time and when the stove, which was supplied by the railway company, was lit in our parlour, the heat of the coal caused its top surface to turn red.

Tommy's donation greatly added to the happiness of Christmas in our house. My mother would light the big oil lamp with its colourful shade on the round table in the centre of the room. This table was covered with a beautiful lace cloth which matched the full length lace window curtains hanging from a bamboo pole. The family sat around the glowing stove listening to records or playing *Ludo* and *Snakes and Ladders*. Christmas day stays in mind as one of the most peaceful and restful days of the year. My father and mother loved it, knowing that they were free of the responsibility of railway duties because no trains ran that day.

Railcar B at Sligo Station. Photo: M.Davies

**4**

# SLIGO-LEITRIM RAIL SYSTEM TO GET LAST WHISTLE TO-NIGHT

Irish Times Reporter

TO-NIGHT a train will pass its last signal, and when it steams to a halt in Sligo station it will mark the closing of a railway system which has served three counties for over three-quarters of a century. At 9.35 o'clock the driver and fireman will step down from the footplate of the engine which brings the last train of the Sligo, Leirim and Northern Counties Railway to its terminal.

Headline from the Irish Times, 30 September 1957

Last Day of the Railway, 30 September 1957 at Glenfarne Station.
Left to right: Pat Clancy, Kevin Wilson, Bernie Gilgunn, Jimmy Keaney and Paddy Denning. Photo: H. Johnston.

# CHAPTER FIFTEEN

# The Last Days of the Railway

Monday, 30 September 1957, was the last official business day in the life of the SL&NCR. That day, I was rostered to work the 11.15am goods train from Sligo Quays. I travelled to the crossing point with the Enniskillen to Sligo goods train i.e. at Glenfarne station. I then boarded the Sligo train for the return journey. On arrival at the Sligo goods depot I handed over my train to the shunters there. This was the last SL&NCR goods train into Sligo after seventy five years of the railway. I rushed home for a wash and meal and then dashed back to the station to witness the arrival of the last passenger train from Enniskillen at 7.20pm.

The platform was crowded. The approach of the train was marked by the deafening noise of fog signals exploding beyond the signal box. Then the dim lights of the engine's two oil-lit headlamps could be seen in the distance. There was great excitement as the train crawled to a stop just yards away from the station's hydraulic buffer stops. One glance at the engine told me that the driver was Gerry O'Connor and the fireman Bertie Hegarty and the nameplate read *Lough Melvin*. Now the engine stood blowing off the surplus steam, which disappeared into the cold air. Slowly the passengers and onlookers drifted away into the night. On the last journey the train was greeted by flickering lights of candles in the windows of the country houses, some high up in the rugged Leitrim hills.

Towards the end of September 1957, when I knew by my roster of duty that my last journey to Enniskillen had come, I decided to say goodbye to all my friends of the SL&NCR and GNR staffs there, before boarding the 1.40pm railcar to Sligo for the final time. When I called into the General Manager's office to collect the correspondence for the stations along the line, the office was like a wakehouse. The faces of the staff told it all – the hurt and dismay at the closure of their beloved railway, through no fault of their own, was so apparent. I said good-bye to each staff member. Many eyes were tear filled and no wonder, since we all enjoyed a great sense of comradeship down the years.

I closed the office door behind me and made my way down the platform to join my railcar for Sligo. As we left Enniskillen many memories came flooding into my mind as did the words of the song "Fare thee well Enniskillen, fare thee well for a while".

I was kept on the company's payroll to the week ending Saturday 5 October as the final wind-down of the railway took place. On Wednesday, 2 October I worked on a special train of empty goods and cattle wagons, which left Sligo at 9.00am for Manorhamilton, shunting and attaching wagons at stations en route. In Manorhamilton I handed over my train to Guard Jimmie McHugh who worked it to Enniskillen. Two days later I worked on the very last train out of Sligo goods depot. As I walked down the branch line to the depot I was occupied with the thought of being unemployed, as work was very hard to get in the 1950s.

I have a very clear memory of that last train, which carried only railway crew. When I arrived at the depot I found it 'made up' on the 'van road', that is the main line from the depot with its many sidings on each side. I checked the train, secured the doors and ensured that all the wagons were double-coupled. (SL&NCR was the only railway company, I know of, who always double-coupled their goods and cattle wagons.) The *Lough Melvin* engine, with driver Jack Connolly and fireman Joe Neilan on board, arrived from its locomotive shed to haul the train. With the branch 'starter' signal in the 'all clear' position, Jack pushed over the engine regulator and the engine responded with a nervous wheel spin. Climbing the steep incline, whistles were exchanged with the depot shunting engine and as we passed the locomotive sheds all the staff came out to wave to us. After crossing the Strandhill road bridge, the women folk of the Treacy Avenue housing estate, which backed onto the line came out into their back gardens and greeted us with a wave of towels and dishcloths.

We stopped at the stations along the way, Ballisodare to pick up staff, Collooney to top up the engine's water tanks and Dromahaire, where the delay was very brief. Then, in Manorhamilton we handed over to another crew – in my case to acting guard Willie Gault (Guard Jimmie McHugh was not available). My guard's equipment was given to foreman John Ward on the instructions of our traffic manager. I kept my train whistle, uniform and other little treasures. Then Jack Connolly, Joe Neilan and myself walked back along the platform to make the return journey to Sligo in a waiting taxi.

Enniskillen Yard, August 1958. Photo: R.K.Walton

The SL&NCR is now part of railway history. Apart from photographs, there is some television footage to perpetuate its memory. In September 1956 a BBC Northern Ireland camera crew recorded passengers boarding the 1.45pm railcar at Enniskillen and continued to take pictures as far as Glenfarne. Paddy Hugh Keaney was the driver and I was the guard. Unfortunately a bad impression of the line was created when a cow came onto the track at the border, just after we left Belcoo. Bernie Gilgunn, who was travelling back to Manorhamilton had to get off the railcar and chase the animal away. I suppose it made good television but we weren't very happy.

We, the workers were proud of our railway. We knew that the trains were important to the people – to all those who depended on it to conduct their business, to school children, shoppers and to the farmers who regulated their day by the times of the passing trains. The smoke from the chimneys of the steam engines, in the opinion of many people, gave some indication of the kind of weather that was to come. If it rose straight up good weather could be expected, but if it didn't gain much height, but swirled close to the ground, bad conditions were on the way.

Enniskillen Yard showing various wagons awaiting disposal.
August 1958. Photo: R.K.Walton

'Enniskillen', 'Lough Erne' and 'Lough Melvin'
in GNR Locomotive shed, Enniskillen, awaiting sale after railway closure.
August 1958. Photo: R.K.Walton

Railway men recalled stories of the many engines old and new which had travelled between Sligo and Enniskillen: – the *Faugh a Ballagh*, the *Glencar*, the *Pioneer*, the *Sligo*, the *Blacklion*, the *Waterford* (which was used for shunting and banking in Collooney), the *Fermanagh*, the *Leitrim* and the *Lurganboy*. The more powerful engines were the *Sir Henry*, the *Lough Gill*, the *Enniskillen*, the *Lough Melvin* and the *Lough Erne*. The *Lissadell* and *Sir Henry* were named for the Gore-Booth family and the *Hazelwood* for Owen Wynne of Hazelwood House, Sligo. The *Lough Melvin* and the *Lough Erne*, received new in 1952, were the last two steam engines to be built by an Irish railway. Indeed the *Lough Erne* is the only engine still to be seen. It is located in Whitehead, Co. Antrim where steam engines and rolling stock are restored. I had the pleasure in September 1993 of seeing it and taking photographs of it. Harold Thompson, Manorhamilton, who has a life-long interest in the railway took Bernie Gilgunn RIP, Pauric McKeon and myself to see it. It is not in the best of shape, but in time will be restored.

Front row: My father James, my mother Annie
Back row: Myself, my sister Kathleen & my brother Tommy.

As for myself, on Tuesday, 8 October 1957 I started work with CIE in the road freight section. In 1991 I retired. Now living in Rose Hill, Sligo, I take life easy, devoting my time to my hobbies of gardening and fishing and helping out with voluntary work.

I have very few railway artifacts in my possession, except a number of personal possessions, photographs and unusually, the original office door from Enniskillen station. It was given to me some years ago by its owner, Leo McGrory and is now restored with a replica nameplate. So I didn't just close the door on a long and happy working life, I brought it home!

# Appendix I

## FINAL DOCUMENTS

Telegraphic Address—
"EGAN" MANORHAMILTON
Tel. 12.
G. F. EGAN,
LOCOMOTIVE, CARRIAGE
AND WAGON
SUPERINTENDENT.

OUR REF. N 57/1.

YOUR REF.

Sligo Leitrim & Northern Counties
Railway Company
Loco Superintendent's Office.

Manorhamilton 28th Sept. 19 57

Dear Mr. Macken,

     I am in receipt of yours of 24th instant.

     Unfortunately the death sentence has now been pronounced and needless to say we are all very despondent, especially as none of us knows if we will get any compensation.

     I do not yet know if there will be an auction or how the disposal of the Company's assets will be effected. The whole question of closing down is most envolved and even our lawyers, who have been threshing it out for some time, at considerable expense to us, do not seem to be able to agree between themselves on some points.

     I enclose some needed rermi etc, but regret I have not got a spare Appendix to the Working Timetable.

                   Yours sincerely,

                   G. F. Egan.

C. R. M. Macken Esq.,
Bank Of Ireland,
Castlerea,
Co. Roscommon.

Saturday 5th Octr. 1957.

Special Rail Car will leave Enniskillen for Sligo at 9.0 a.m.
Florencecourt dep. 9.15 a.m. Belcoo dep. 9.35 a.m. Glenfarne
dep. 9.55 a.m. Manorhamilton dep. 10.45 a.m. Dromahair dep.
11.5 a.m. Ballintogher dep. 11.15 a.m. Collooney dep. 11.30 a.m.
Ballysodare dep. 11.35 a.m. Sligo arr. 11.50 a.m.     This Car
will return from Sligo to Enniskillen at 2.0 p.m.

Belcoo and Glenfarne to arrange Customs attendance for above
services and ascertain running either by telegraph or telephone
so as to advise Officers of time to attend at station.

Station Premises etc.

Station Masters to see Station premises, platforms, etc. are
cleaned and all litter gathered up.

Cash Bags.

Cash Bags will not now be returned to stations on Monday 30th inst.

Payment of Wages.

Further to my circular of 23rd instant; it has now been decided
to pay wages due for W.E. 5th October on that day. Insurance
Cards will also be available. Traffic staff and Road Supervisor
to note accordingly.

                         H. E. TAYLOR
                         Traffic Manager.

Telegrams: " TAYLOR, RAILWAY, ENNISKILLEN."
Telephone · ENNISKILLEN 2027.
## SLIGO, LEITRIM AND NORTHERN COUNTIES RAILWAY.

H. E. TAYLOR
TRAFFIC MANAGER

Traffic Manager's Office,
Enniskillen.

My Ref :

Your Ref :


TO WHOM IT MAY CONCERN:

This is to certify that

    MICHAEL J. HAMILTON

has been employed with this Company since
1945 and has held the grade of  GUARD
for some time.

He applied himself to the work and took
a keen interest in the performance of his
duties in which he was proficient.

He is a man of excellent character and gave
every satisfaction.  His severance with
this Company is consequent on the closing
down of our services.

I shall always be glad to hear of his
success.

H. E. Taylor.

TRAFFIC MANAGER.


26th September, 1957.

SLIGO, LEITRIM & NORTHERN COUNTIES RAILWAY.

General Manager's office,
ENNISKILLEN, 20th Septr., 1957.

Owing to the discontinuance of Rail Services through
Enniskillen as on and from 1st October, 1957, this
Company will be unable to operate its Rail and Road
services after 30th September.

I have been instructed by the Directors to give you
Notice terminating your employment with the Company
after the completion of your rostered turn of duty on
Saturday, 5th October, 1957.

The necessity of doing so is very much regretted, but it
will be recognized the Directors have no alternative, and
I have been asked to convey their appreciation of your
loyal and faithful service to the Company.

Your Insurance Card will be handed you along with payment
of wages on 10th October.

Consequent on this Notice, possession of any house or
premises occupied by an employee by reason of his or her
employment with the Company will be required.

GENERAL MANAGER.

Guard M.J.Hamilton
Slip

---

Friday 4th Octr. 1957.

On Friday 4th October, special train will leave Sligo for
Enniskillen at 9.0 a.m. (Nine a.m.) with this Company's empty
wagons (housetop, flat and cattle), Vans, foreign wagons and
Company's coal on hands at Sligo, picking up similar rolling stock
at Ballysodare. Local wagons to be placed on siding at Collooney.
Dromahair to forward similarly to Manorhamilton. Glenfarne and Belcoo
to forward similarly to Enniskillen. Company's coal to Manorhamilton.
Foreign wagons to Enniskillen for G.N.R. transfer. This special will
be worked by Guard Hamilton to Manorhamilton thence to Enniskillen
by Guard McHugh. ENGINE STABLES IN ENNISKILLEN.

# DANIEL MORRISSEY & SONS LTD

## M.I.A.A.

DIRECTORS: DANIEL MORRISSEY. MARY MORRISSEY. ANTHONY MORRISSEY. LIAM MORRISSEY.

## AUCTIONEERS AND VALUERS

**MERRION BUILDING**
LR. MERRION STREET
### DUBLIN

TELEPHONE 65781 - 5 LINES

6th April, 1959.

Our Ref. OM/BMcC.
Machinery Division.

Mr. C. R. M. Macken,
Arus Cruain,
Knockroe,
Castlerea,
CO. ROSCOMMON.

Dear Sir,          Re:   Sale of Sligo-Leitrim & N. C. Railway Co.

We acknowledge with thanks receipt of your letter dated the 4th instant, together with postal order for 2/6d. We will have pleasure in forwarding you catalogue for the above auction next week, when it becomes available from the Printers.

Yours faithfully,

DANIEL MORRISSEY & SONS LTD.

DIRECTOR.

# Appendix II

## LEVEL CROSSING GATEHOUSES 1957

The level crossing gatehouses were numbered in ascending order from Enniskillen Station which was situated in the townland of Breandrum but didn't provide any living accommodation. Office staff only worked there.

**No 1 Level Crossing**
Townland of Mullylogan; occupier John McTernan.
**No. 2 Level Crossing**
Townland of Drumkeen; occupier P. Nolan.
**No 3. Level Crossing**
Townland of Mullaghey; occupier B. Gault.
**No. 4 Florencecourt Station**
Townland of Derryscob; occupier Robin Gault Acting station - master. (Archie Burns had retired).
**No. 5 Level Crossing**
 Townland of : Corryglass; occupier  J. Scales.
                        Abohill Halt: occupier P. McAlone.
**No 6 Belcoo Station**
Townland of Belcoo East; occupier Freddie Monaghan.
**No 7 Level Crossing**
Townland of Killinagh; occupier Ed Keaney (Sr).
**No 8 Level Crossing**
Townland of Killcarney; occupier Frank Kelly.
**No 9 Level Crossing**
Townland of Thornhill; occupier J. Packenham.
**No 10 Level Crossing**
Townland of Roo; occupier P. Packenham.
**No 11 Level Crossing**
Townland of Correvan; occupier Ed Keaney (Jr.)

**No 12 Level Crossing**
Townland of Brockagh; occupier J. Darcy.
Glenfarne Station in townland of Brockagh. M. Walsh was the Road
Passenger Supervisor. P. Denning was the Station Master. He stayed
in lodgings in O Rourkes, near the station.
**No 13 Level Crossing**
Townland of Cornacloy; occupier J. Williamson.
**No 14 Level Crossing**
Kilmakerril Halt; occupier Michael Clancy.
**No 15 Level Crossing**
Townland of Lisnagroagh; occupier Paddy Williamson.
**No 16 Level Crossing**
Townland of Cherrybrook; occupier Peter McKeon.
**No 17 Manorhamilton Station**
Townland of Donaghmore; Station Master J. Magee. He did not live in
the station but owned the Manor Hotel in town.
**No 18 Level Crossing**
Townland of Cleen; occupier Thomas Fowley.
**No 19 Level Crossing**
Townland of Killinama; occupier Edward Lambe.
**No 20 Level Crossing**
Townland of Edergole; occupier  Charles Carty.
**No 21 Level Crossing**
Townland of Derrybrisk; occupier James Hamilton.
**No 22 Level Crossing**
Townland of Tobernania; occupier  John Loughlin.
**No 23 Level Crossing**
Townland of Aitveiled ; occupier Michael Carney.
**No 24 Ballintogher Station**
Townland of Rathangan; occupier  Paddy Farmer.
**No 25 Level Crossing**
Townland of Woodfield; occupier James Bredin.
**No 26 Level Crossing**
Townland of  Kilross ; occupier John Conlon.
**No 27 Level Crossing**

Townland of Castledargan; occupier Michael Drumm.

**Ballygawley Halt:** had shelter accommodation for train passengers but no other buildings.

**No 28 Collooney Station**

Townland of Markree; There was no living accommodation here. The Station Master, P. Denning was provided with a house in St. Mary's Green, Collooney.

In this year 1997 of the the 23 level crossing gatehouses, 3 are demolished, 11 are still occupied and beautifully restored; 9 are unoccupied. Of the 8 stations, 2 are demolished 4 are occupied and 2 are unoccupied.

# Appendix III

## THE HALTS TO PICK UP
## AND SET DOWN PASSENGERS

There were five halts along the line. They were used quite a lot by schoolchildren. Abohill Halt was situated $8^1/_4$ miles from Enniskillen on the 'down' side of the line. The platform was about ninety feet long and there was a corrugated iron shelter for passengers. It was opened in summer 1886.

Killmakerrill Halt was sited $21^3/_4$ miles from Enniskillen on the 'up' side of the line and it was opened on 28th July 1929. The gatekeeper, whose house was sited opposite the halt, set his signal at 'danger' to inform the traindriver if there were passengers waiting to board the 7.20pm steam train ex-Enniskillen.

Lisgorman Halt was situated $29^1/_2$ miles from Enniskillen. It was opened in 1887 but was closed again in 1917 and the platform removed. The main reason for the closure was that steam-trains from Sligo experienced some difficulty restarting on the gradient at this point. However with the introduction of railcars the company opened a stopping point in Lisgorman in 1940. The platform was not rebuilt, since passengers using two tiered steps could board the railcar from ground level.

Ballintogher Halt was 36 miles from Enniskillen. It was opened around January 1883. The platform was on the 'down' side and there was a corrugated shelter, to which a goods store of similar construction was added in 1909. Ballintogher also had a level crossing and gatehouse, where the haltkeeper lived. He operated the gates and issued tickets to boarding passengers. The postman also called here with his P.O mails for Sligo. Inward goods and Guinness stout was transhipped from the 'up' Sligo Goods Train – goods trains from Enniskillen would never stop here as it would be almost impossible to start a heavy goods train due to the steep gradient heading towards Sligo. As in Killmakerrill, the haltkeeper set his signal at 'danger' to inform the train driver that there were passengers awaiting the 7.20pm steam train ex-Enniskillen.

Ballygawley Halt was situated by an underbridge at 39³/₄ miles from Enniskillen. Opened in 1887, the platform was on the 'down' side and had a corrugated iron shelter. Passengers intending to get off here would notify the guard at Dromahaire station. In 1956 the 7.20pm steam train from Enniskillen ceased to stop here.

A regular passenger who alighted at Ballygawley was a local lad named Kieran Horan. He worked in TA Golden's in Manorhamilton. Each Saturday night he travelled home taking his bicycle with him. At Dromahaire I usually took his bicycle from the guards van and put it in the carriage compartment, making it handy for unloading in the darkness on arrival at Ballygawley. Like other halts, there was no lighting provided in Ballygawley – the light from the carriage was deemed sufficient.